TÀPIES

Victòria Combalia Dexeus

TÀPIES

RIZZOLI
NEW YORK

First published in the United States of America in 1990 by

RIZZOLI INTERNATIONAL PUBLICATIONS, INC.

300 Park Avenue South, New York, NY 10010

© 1989 Ediciones Polígrafa, S. A.
Translated by Kenneth Lyons

Library of Congress Cataloging-in-Publication Data

Combalía Dexeus, Victoria, 1952-
     Tàpies / Victoria Combalía Dexeus.
        p.   cm.
     Includes bibliographical references.
     ISBN 0-8478-1197-2
     1. Tàpies, Antoni, 1923-   —Criticism and interpretation.
I. Title.
N7113.T3C83   1990   89-63959
709'.2—dc20   CIP

Printed and bound in Spain by La Polígrafa, S. A.
Parets del Vallès (Barcelona)
Dep. Leg. B. 44.231 - 1989

CONTENTS

ANTONI TÀPIES (Barcelona, 1969)

"Anything that has been explained ceases to interest us."
Nietzsche:
Beyond Good and Evil

"It is our imagination that persists in clothing things; but the things themselves are divinely naked."
Marguerite Yourcenar:
Alexis or The Treatise of the Useless Combat

Introduction

One of the arguments most frequently employed against abstract art is an argument of comparison: traditional art, it tells us, represents characters known to us or, at least, believable, and its appearance imitates that of reality. Traditional art is, therefore, understandable. It is true, indeed, that in the art of earlier ages we can distinguish figures and we are told stories, but neither is this appearance so natural as may seem at first sight nor are all its images copies of the external world. In order to understand the allegories of the Mannerists, art lovers of the day first needed to know the complex significance of their symbols; to understand Poussin an acquaintance with mythology was essential; and there are some pictures, like the Mona Lisa or Velázquez's *Maids of Honor*, that are still open to a great variety of interpretations. Paintings by the "old masters" may be admired for their technique, their composition or their coloring, but we cannot really grasp their ultimate meaning if we do not also possess a thorough knowledge of the period, the aims pursued by the painters, their iconography and even the external history of the picture itself.

As for the theory that art must be a reproduction of reality, this is a principle with a long, complex and densely nuanced history. Aristotle, founder of the doctrine of art imitating nature, held that reality could be represented as it is, but above all better (in tragedy) or worse (in comedy) than it is. This implies two considerable manipulations or distortions of reality which, in painting, were to lead to idealization or expressionism. The Renaissance artists, for instance — although with the invention of perspective and the gradual perfecting of modelling they succeeded in producing images that were much closer to what the eye actually sees — alternated direct perception with the idealization of attitudes and characters, a feature borrowed from the classical Greek art which they admired so much. The art of the Renaissance, like any other, was also subject to conventions and survivals of tradition; but its great discoveries, such as that of geometrical perspective, were to be "superseded" by a representation of space which in later centuries was to succeed in giving form to the sensation of the air that passes between solid volumes: aerial perspective.

It will be as well to remember, moreover, that what is still for many people a model of perfection — the classicism of Raphael — did not long remain inviolate. The later works of Michelangelo, for instance, do not concentrate on producing a perfect anatomy or an idealized beauty, but rather attempt above all to *express* a personal — religious — conflict through the distortion of the figures. As in his

7

case, there are many styles that challenge direct observation on the one hand or an ideal canon on the other. The so-called primitives arts, for instance, prefer to show the permanent shape of things — their conceptual images, so to speak — and their appearance is therefore schematic or synthesized. And all expressionist artists, from El Greco to Picasso, likewise distort the "natural" vision of objects in their endeavor to transmit a subjective view of them.

There is no such thing, therefore, as a single "normal" or truthful representation. As the historian Alois Riegl said, "each style has its own conception of nature"; which is as much as to say, among other things, that each age "sees" in a different way. These changes do not come about abruptly; in each period there are some conventions which have become established as the prevailing style and then there are certain artists who break with them, thus establishing a new code which in turn becomes established as a tradition. These artists, however, are not starting out from scratch either; philosophical or religious ideas and changes in the composition of society have their influence on them, however indirectly. It would be inconceivable, for instance, to discuss the achievements of *quattrocento* illusionism without making some allusion to the apparition of a proto-bourgeoisie whose positive mentality in business affairs stimulated the development of a scientific spirit. Nor can we consider Michelangelo's profound anguish, or his mysticism, without taking into account the moral trauma that the Reformation meant for the Catholic Church.

All changes in style, then, presuppose changes in the interests, values and concepts of their age. But if we are to understand the irruption of modern art, which is what concerns us particularly here as a preliminary to understanding the art of Tàpies, the example of the struggle against academic art is the most relevant of all.

Though classicism, of course, is just one style among many others, it is undeniable that it was of fundamental importance to the teachings of the Academy. This institution, which was first conceived as a center not only for the teaching but also for the intellectual recognition of the plastic arts, was regarded as the ultimate authority from the 17th century onwards, though by the 19th century its system of rules and precepts might also have been described as repressive. Among these precepts those of the idealized human figure, the narration of a noble and elevated "story" and the superiority of drawing to color may be regarded as the most important. But what had at first been a humanistic ideal — and indeed, as far as artistic criteria were concerned, rather a stimulus than an imposition — gradually became an outmoded pattern, a collection of incomplete, humdrum clichés. It need not surprise us, then, that the most restless and questing spirits among the artists of the 19th century resisted the influence of the Academy in their desire to recover, curiously enough, something of the empirical vision of the *quattrocento*. The "innocent gaze" (to use a phrase coined by Ruskin) was a basic element in the achievements of such artists as Constable, Courbet and the Impressionists; insofar as such a gaze is impossible, however, these achievements inevitably collided with the established canons of their time. Constable — to some extent the creator of the modern landscape — was severely critized for painting his meadows green; everybody, of course, saw them that color, but the conventions of landscape painting decreed that gray and dun tones should be placed in the foreground (even for trees and meadows) and graduated tones of silvery blue in the background, in order to suggest greater depth. Much the same thing happened to the Impressionists, who were censured not only on the score of their apparent contempt for drawing — something which the Impressionist painters knew only too well — but also for the brilliance of their colors, which the critics considered excessive. To the modern eye, however, in comparison with the luminous colors of the Impressionist school the pictures of earlier periods tend to seem too dark.

The desire for veracity and visual "honesty" instead of the clichés of convention — which was also a desire for moral veracity as against the rhetoric and moralizing of the academicians — led these 19th-century artists to turn to styles other than the classic ones in search of support for their ideas. Hence the consideration accorded from then onward to popular art, medieval art and, above all, the primitive arts, which were to have such a great influence on the majority of modern artists: on Gauguin and Picasso, on German Expressionism, on the Surrealists and on Abstract Expressionism in America, to mention only a few instances. There is, of course, a great difference between primitive and modern art: what in the former belongs to an established world of collective beliefs and symbols, in modern art takes the form of an individual expression based on a free, experimental attitude to forms, as Meyer Schapiro has so rightly pointed out. Besides, the uncompromising subjectivism of the modern spirit is a consequence of the freedom brought by the French Revolution and by the critical spirit of the Romantics, already profoundly at variance with an age in which positive, material values prevailed over those of the spirit.

This dissatisfaction with the present on the part of artists and intellectuals has its origin in some of the profound social transformations that have helped to shape the contemporary world. The freedom gained during the French Revolution became, in fact, a freedom that particularly favored the enrichment of a new bourgeoisie — whose taste in art, moreover, was best satisfied by contemporary practitioners of familiar styles and the picturesque. This was a development that entailed a progressive decline in commissions from the ruling classes, forcing the artist henceforth to rely more and more on the representation of his work at official Salons and exhibitions, which were subject to the academic rules. To these circumstances must be added the fact that the invention and rapid popularization of photography meant the disappearance of tasks formerly the province of painters, such as portraits, miniatures and the description of places and events. This, it is true, gave the artist much greater freedom for experimenting and even resulted, psychologically, in a new ascetic pride characterizing those who felt they belonged to the avantgarde; but this feeling was inescapably counterbalanced by incomprehension and isolation as far as the general public was concerned. Attempts were to be made to remedy this situation in Utopian experiments like the Bauhaus or Russian Constructivism; since the 1950s, however, the higher level of education in the arts, museum purchases and the spectacular boom in the art market have brought about, at least in developed countries, a widespread acceptance of modern art.

Abstract art

Though the conditions of art changed around the end of the 19th century with the gradual liberation of the artist from his subjection to conventional themes, this does not mean that such familiar old concepts as representation and expression have ceased to be propounded in radically new ways. At first sight the process seems a reductive one, eliminating all identifiable references to the external world — as in the case of Mondrian's series of trees, for instance — to a point at which these signs no longer appear able to communicate with the viewer. This reductionism is indeed evident, but we should also bear in mind the simultaneous operation of an endeavor to "regenerate" the basic elements of plastic language: color, line and volume. The avant-garde artists of the early 20th century felt only horror for the illusionism of traditional art, in which they saw deceit and motives extraneous to painting itself. They had, however, an immense faith in their ability to invent their own pictorial structures and create an art "without a subject," comparable in some ways to musical creation. Apollinaire, as long ago as 1908, was constantly speaking about the purity and self-referential nature of painting, a vision that might be summed up in the opinion expressed by Theo van Doesburg in 1930: "A painting must be constructed with plastic elements alone, that is to say with planes and colors. A plastic element possesses no other significance than itself and a painting, therefore, means nothing but itself."

This type of reasoning, however, is essentially programmatic and, as we all know, any manifesto must be partial if it is to have force at all. Abstract art, in fact, is something much more profound than a mere combination of forms, colors or textures; even when it is proposed as an experiment in the representation of banal objects — as might be argued in the case of Cubism — these distortions are a response to a new way of perceiving the world, and their results gradually come

9

to influence our own way of seeing it. Cubism as practiced by Picasso and Braque is, in effect, a permanent struggle with the motif, breaking the object into multiple planes in the first stage and then putting it together again in accordance with an idea already independent of direct observation. In analytical Cubism the table, the chair and the guitar no longer have the clarity that characterized Renaissance art, but a new material consistency made up of textures and allusions (which was why Picasso himself said that this new consistency was like the aroma of a scent). The most worthwhile part of this school's contribution to art had nothing to do with reductionism but was concerned, quite to the contrary, with the tensions between the various levels of reality created, from their designation on a basis of textures or outlines to the details in *trompe l'œil* or the inclusion of collage. It is, if you like, a new version of realism, a version approached through different formal solutions that were to lead to many different ways of representing things in 20th-century art.

There are, however, other forms of abstract art in which the images emerge from the artist's mental world and are presented to some extent as the system of symbols of an intellectual universe aspiring to be taken for a Utopian model. When Mondrian, for instance, painted his work in what appears to be simply a set of verticals, horizontals and primary colors, there was behind him a philosophical conception of the world based on theosophy, and his ambition was to create a new order, a new equilibrium between contrary forces (matter/spirit, male/female) until he could finally achieve purity in itself.

Thus, while the Cubist solution is a representation at least *based on* reality, the one proposed by Mondrian may be included in a series of idealistic conceptions which considered that over and above what was merely visible and circumstantial there were certain higher principles, what we might call transcendent archetypes.

Reactions of this sort can be more readily understood when we remember that in the first twenty years of this century the postulates of modern physics, with their equation of matter and energy and their "discovery" of the divisibility of the atom, impressed the world so much that they positively discredited tangible reality. The so-called laws of nature, too, lost their former validity with the crisis of causality; the age-old certainty of the universe was yielding place to laws based on probability alone.

Nor should we, finally, underrate the influence of certain ideas of the Romantics, such as that of the artist's subjectivity filtering external sensations. It is one's own sensitivity that gives an "inner sound" to form and color, according to Kandinsky, for whom ultramarine was velvety, whereas blue-green was "hard and dry." There is nothing to prevent us from seeing it otherwise: among other characteristics, abstract art includes the viewer more completely, for he is less constrained now by the subject or episode that is compulsory in all traditional art.

Thus abstract art can create new guidelines for representing reality, inventing it afresh in a totally different form or distorting it through sensations and feelings. It can fragment it, re-create it, imagine it, but in the final analysis abstract art will do to reality what all artists have done: interpret it.

Tàpies: childhood, adolescence and the Surrealist period

It may be extremely biased to explain a painter's work as the result of his temperament or his recorded biography, but it is no less so to deny the importance of his human and social background. While the Renaissance popularized the legend of artists as curious, atypical personalities (anecdotes about whom were often exaggerated to make them seem even more incredible), our own century has seen the acceptance of Wölfflin's concept of a history of art without names, a history in which everything is supposed to hang together in a collective formal process. But the fact remains that the relationship between an artist's work and his life is an extraordinarily complex one. In some cases it is the programmatic element, the intellectual projection, that prevails, while in others, especially since Romanticism, the work becomes the externalization of a subject, the plastic expression of his inner life, his obsessions and his phantoms. His painting is then established as a redoubt of freedom (against the academic canons) and, in some cases, as a "lay" exorcism; Goya would, perhaps, be the best example of this. But the really great artist does not stop at any merely therapeutical stage; his greatness lies in leaping over the gap between what is private to him and what is capable of communicating profound human problems.

In my opinion certain experiences from Tàpies' childhood and adolescence were of decisive importance in the formation of the repertory of themes that make up his basic artistic vocabulary. Even if we knew nothing of these experiences, his work would be equally valid for its plastic quality and its power to address problems that affect not only a generation but the whole of mankind in the western world today: the collapse of certain values undermined by Franco's dictatorship in Spain; the fragmentation and artificiality of modern man. But once we are aware of these youthful experiences, most of which are described in the artist's memoirs, we are in a better position to understand his motivations and even specific themes in his work — as is also the case with Picasso, another artist whose autobiography, from the 1930s on, is fundamental to such understanding.

This section on Tàpies's childhood and upbringing, therefore, cannot be reduced to a mere string of more or less anecdotal events. In his endeavor to remember, any artist writing his memoirs will choose what he considers most significant; he usually adds, however, intellectual justifications which, though they may be important in his life as a man, do not necessarily affect his work as a painter. From all this material those who study the artist's work must decide what seems most relevant or significant in each of these two aspects.

Antoni Tàpies was born in Barcelona on 13th December 1923, in a bourgeois family of liberal and Catalanists sympathies that had played some part in the cultural and political life of the city. His maternal great-grandfather, Eudald Puig, who was a bookseller and publisher, had been a deputy mayor during the mayoralty of Rius i Taulet. His grandfather on the same side, who was a friend of Prat de la Riba and Cambó, occupied the same position as his father and, as acting mayor, received King Alfonso XIII of Spain on his visit to Barcelona in 1908. Thus his daughter — Maria Puig i Guerra, Tàpies's mother — grew up with an emphatic consciousness of her social position; she was rather timid and a fervent Catholic, with a temperament totally contrary to that of her husband, Josep Tàpies, the painter's father. Josep Tàpies has been described by his son as an extremely sociable but absentminded man, nervous and anticlerical; before the Civil War he had a law office of the highest repute. He had always been a supporter of the Republic, but after the excesses of the war he became more and more conservative. This was quite a common change of heart among Catalan bourgeois liberals, though in the case of Tàpies's father many of the contradictions of the postwar years were particularly evident: on the one hand, he watched the rise to new riches of some of his friends, which made him feel isolated and depressed; on the other, the fact that he had collaborated with the Generalitat (Autonomous Government of Catalonia) exposed him to some measure of official disapproval, which in turn brought him serious financial difficulties.

Among the things that Tàpies remembers most vividly from his childhood are the family's constant moves from one house to another in order to satisfy his mother's ideas of what was due to her social status; then there was his own shyness, the horror inspired by his primary schooling at the Loreto convent and his feeling of isolation among his classmates. He remembers the smells and the old furniture in flats occupied by the family in Barcelona's Gothic Quarter, and the humiliation of having to submit to his paternal grandmother's insistence that children should frequently be given enemas to "keep them regular." The decrepitude and the physiological intimacies that were to appear so frequently in his work are all associated with unpleasant memories of this kind; memories that only much later he succeeded in reproducing in the form of rejection or poetry.

This childhood and early adolescence is that of an inner world tormented by religious conflicts (his father and others in the family had studied at religious seminaries) and by the fear and fascination aroused by everything sinful or secret, but also influenced by his discovery of eastern philosophy and classical music. His

greatest pleasure consisted of using his frequent ailments to avoid his classes and stay at home, reading or drawing. He was always a sickly child: first he had typhus, then brucellosis and, at the age of eighteen, tuberculosis, the first symptom of which was a severe attack of tachycardia which brought him very close to death. The Civil War, coinciding with his puberty, brought air raids and hunger; but it also brought a degree of freedom unheard-of for a bourgeois child at that time, together with experiences that remained fixed in his memory and were to be represented, in one way or another, in his work. The memory of a sexual exhibition — young girls with their legs wide apart, surrounded by a group of slavering adolescents — may have been the genesis of a work entitled *Composition with Figures* (a), in which a little boy is looking directly at the pudenda of a woman covering her breasts with her hands; the letter M, moreover, so often found in Tàpies's painting, has on several occasions been interpreted as a formal metaphor for wide-open legs. Another of Tàpies' memories is of a Francoist patriotic celebration held in some dilapidated premises in 1939, at which a young man decided to have a bath in icy water, placing himself with his feet and hands at the four corners of the bathtub: "as though he had been crucified on that tub, and in such peculiar circumstances, near a burial mound... that extraordinary scene impressed me deeply," says the painter in his memoirs.

Later, too, he was to recall the repulsion aroused by those precocious visits to brothels: "that flesh seemed to belong to women who were already decrepit; it repelled me much more than it attracted me. Sometimes it made me think of the weary body of my own mother, seen by accident, or of some old servants — the smells, too, in this latter case."

His reading ranged from Tolstoy, Dickens and Dostoevsky to Unamuno, Nietzsche, Poe, Wilde, Stendhal, Proust and Gide. At the sanatorium in Puig d'Olena, in 1942, he totally lost his religious faith and began to make a thorough study of Hindu philosophy. Later on he was to experience strange hallucinations, "which made me see my body on the inside, but as though it contained the whole Universe." These semi-pantheistic experiences stemming from his own person were, however, a source of anguish: "at that time.... I often saw myself reflected in the big mirror in my wardrobe door and sometimes, if the door was ajar, I found myself face to face with that pale child sitting on the bed and gazing at me with eyes that always had rings under them." His earliest drawings include many self-portraits that show him with a tortured or visionary look; the wardrobe and the mirror were later to figure frequently in his painting.

His initiation into art — though his father thought it a preposterous idea and insisted on his studying law at the same time — was one way to salvation; another was his first meeting with Teresa Barba, who was later to become his wife. Due to the Francoist regime's veto on all avant-garde art, the Spanish painting scene in the forties was depressingly mediocre, with a proliferation of vaguely impressionist work, cosily undemanding realism (idyllic or picturesque landscapes, still lifes) and a certain populism deriving from the early 20th-century Catalan school known as *Noucentisme*. But thanks to the famous special issue of the magazine *D'Ací i d'Allà*, published in 1934, Tàpies already knew the names and work of the most important representatives of the first European avant-garde movements. There should be, he thought, a higher form of art, one nearer to poetry, an art that would replace the Hegelian God with wisdom or knowledge. Art was a moral option, an attitude to life; all avant-garde movements accept this premise, but it was particularly from Surrealism that Tàpies was to take the first consequences. That movement's interest in the subconscious mind, in everything magical and alogical, attracted him as a challenge to established morality — he was likewise attracted by the deep-seated angst of Van Gogh, some of whose works he copied. In 1945, while staying at the monastery of El Miracle, Tàpies started to draw feverishly in a style unmistakably marked by the Surrealist influence.

These early works reveal a strong mystical, pantheistic and magical sense. There is a series of self-portraits, for instance, in which the body merges into nature, thrusting its feet into the earth or entering the water, with the sun, the moon and the stars all appearing at the same time; the whole radiates the same mental energy, the cosmos is One. It might also be argued that this communication with the whole

(b) Tàpies: *Drawing*, 1944.

of the animal and plant kingdom survives, though reduced to abstract signs, in his later work. Cirlot, for instance, interprets the parallel wavy striations of the "matter" pictures as symbols of water or of the elementary movements of the reptiles which are also frequently found in prehistoric pottery.

In these early drawings the human figure is placed centrally and statically, as in certain kinds of archaic and primitive art; there are ritual scenes, scenes of initiation, visionary scenes. The eyes may be completely closed, one closed and the other open or both turned upwards, expressing psychic states of concentration or clairvoyance. Feet and hands are likewise of great importance and the naked body also appears as the symbol of a state unconstrained by rules, a more purely animal state. As with the generation of abstract painters working in America some years before, primitive art and Surrealism provided the bridge that was indispensable to any revolt against academicism and the western rationalist tradition. And, as occurs with the very first works of Pollock, Rothko or Gorky, these early drawings by Tàpies are more interesting because of this context of the break with tradition than for what they are in themselves. In their style they reproduce some of the devices of *art brut* (the art of madmen and dropouts), such as the representation of mental energy by means of repeated lines and motifs, and the covering of the whole surface with drawing. But there are also echoes of Picasso and Picabia, of the latter particularly in the androgynous figure in a drawing done in 1944 (b). Looking back over Tàpies' career, it is interesting to see that the importance of symmetry in his more mature work is also a pared down continuation of that to be found in his earliest drawings, the result of the influence of archaic art. Hans Platschek seems to be alluding to this when he says that the vertical axes and the symmetrical arrangement of Tàpies' pictures might be related to the images we find in Max Ernst's work during what is called his totemic period.

In spite of their having a powerful narrative content, Tàpies wanted each of his works to be an independent plastic object, charged with mental energy. "The value of the work as a presence," he tells us, "has to be as strong as that of a talisman or icon." That is to say, they were supposed to speak for themselves but to convey not only mystery but also a sense of force and power. Worth recalling in this connection are the words of Picasso, as recorded by Malraux, after the great painter's visit to the Musée du Trocadero: "The works of negro art were intended to intercede, to mediate.... They were against everything — against the unknown, against evil spirits.... I realized what the black races used those sculptures for.... They were arms for helping people not to fall once more under the influence of the spirits, arms for helping them to be independent. They were instruments.... The spirits or the subsconscious (though this was not yet so widely spoken of as today), emotion — it is all the same. I realized why I was a painter." For an artist like Picasso, who has generally been studied for the purely formal aspects of his break with tradition, this statement is extremely thought-provoking and alludes, once again, to that "lay" exorcism of which I have already spoken.

Thanks to his interest in the avant-garde, in the world of magic and in the music of Wagner, Tàpies soon became a close friend of the poet Joan Brossa, whose portrait he painted in 1950 — though he remodeled this picture in 1970 with the addition of signs that "erase" the earlier academic handling and an enigmatic sponge at the level of the heart (Fig. 4). At that time Brossa was already acquainted with Foix and Miró, two of the most outstanding representatives of the prewar avant-garde movements. It was Brossa and Tàpies, together with Arnau Puig, Modest Cuixart and Joan Ponç, and with Tharrats as their publisher, who founded the review *Dau al Set* (1948-1951), encouraged by that great promoter of modern art, Joan Prats. Surrealism was the style most generally favored by the *Dau al Set* painters, but they also devoted time and energy to spreading the fame of Miró, Klee, Picabia, Schönberg; to discussing jazz and Gaudí; to a lively interest in the occult and the demoniac, as well as in modern psychology (Freud was still little known in Spain then; in any case it was the theories of Jung that were later to make a great impression on Tàpies). The oracle Brossa wrote for Tàpies on the occasion of his exhibition at the Galeries Laietanes in 1950 is a good example of the ritual, Nietzschean tone so noticeable in his writing at that time: "To touch the top of a hillock with one's hand: is not that a good omen? After this, behold,

13

(c) Klee: *17, Mad,* 1923.

(d) Tàpies: *Political Archeology,*
1952.

the day will come when there is a new age of men for man, and there will be an end to pride. And on that day the eggs will abandon the shelter of the stones and boiling saliva will fall from men's mouths.''

This was the time, to be sure, when Tàpies was producing landscapes of an apocalyptic, mysterious kind. Previously, however, between 1945 and 1947, he had done works with a tremendous amount of pigment, in which primitive faces and hands emerge from the striated treatment of the paste itself, as in Van Gogh's work. At that time, too, he did collages with paper, threads and other unconventional materials, initially motivated by an urge to provoke but certainly not so negative as has sometimes been suggested. "Pain and wretchedness are evident here, but perhaps with a certain feeling of tenderness, like a sadness, a compassion, felt for all that is most humble, with a desire for essentiality that enters fully into the world of positive facts." This is what the painter himself has said of them, and it is an opinion that is perfectly applicable to all his work. There are some of these experiments which basically constitute gestures expressing his break with "noble" materials (Fig. 1), others in which a natural sense of composition appears, as in the 1947 *Collage of the Crosses* (Fig. 3). In *"Grattage" on Cardboard* (Fig. 2), done in the same year, a figure whose features recall those seen in children's painting is given a body formed by holes scraped out of the cardboard support, so that the base material is not just another plastic element but an expressive one. The light, too, helps to bring about the desired blend of the real and the unreal.

The mysterious light, with spots or illuminated areas in the midst of a great darkness (reminiscent, incidentally, of Turner and Rembrandt), appears again in certain compositions painted between 1948 and 1952, with silhouette-like figures and signs that are like references to Klee and Miró (c and d); these points of light give depth to the composition, which is even further enhanced by the scenography we find in the works painted in 1950 and 1951. The most clean-stripped of these, with their architectural elements, remind one of the dream spaces of the Surrealist painter Yves Tanguy. When they are filled with recognizable elements, these objects are charged with restlessness by their illogical juxtaposition and their alteration of perspective, as we see in *Nourishment* (Fig. 5) or in *The Legerdemain of Wotan* (Fig. 6), a title evoking that Norse god, magician and poet, who stole hydromel (the drink some have regarded as the origin of life) from the Wagnerian poet-hero. We should remember that an admiration for Wagner, though fairly widespread in Catalonia, was in the fifties regarded as little short of a provocation by intellectuals of the left, for in those days he was associated with Nazism.

In 1949 and 1950 the more forward-looking artists were raising the question of valid solutions for political preoccupations in relation to modern art. As in the case of the American painters ten years earlier, their dilemma consisted of deciding which option in the plastic arts would be in line with the most critical political position of the time, which was that of the Marxists. The personality of João Cabral, Brazilian consul in Barcelona and also a poet, had a decisive influence on Brossa (who was to write plays with something of a social-realist content, though poetical) and on Tàpies. The latter accepted the dictum that the alternative to the formalism of modern art would have to be "a rediscovery of the world of men," but not Cabral's dismissal of abstract art. It was at this moment of transition that Tàpies did his *Bank Note Collage* (Fig. 7), which might be viewed as the explicit interpretation of one of the artificialities of the modern age: the material value of things expressed, as it has been since the end of the 18th century, by the conventional standard of bank notes, here stained with red ink. The notes, moreover, form an X, a sign that was to be repeated frequently in later works. In 1952 and 1953 Tàpies embarked on a series of works — *The Amphora* (Fig. 8) is surely not the best example — in which some measure of geometric abstraction makes an appearance, though mysteriousness is maintained by the use of such elements as the moon or the unreal lights.

From 1953 onward Tàpies gradually stripped his art of everything anecdotal and the last vestiges of Surrealism, giving it instead a mature style of its own. This, of course, was no sudden change but an extremely intelligent refining process in which the mystery of his earlier works, until then still subordinated to the "story," was turned into ambiguity by the way he treated his material; and this treatment, in turn, had its origin in those early experiments, which ceased to be mere gestures and became confrontations with directly plastic problems. A contributory factor to this, as the artist himself recalls, was the great freedom and sense of experimentation that he saw in Miró.

A painting like *White with Red Stains* (Fig. 9), done in 1954, is already a consummate work of art. Thus, at the age of thirty, Tàpies had attained a plastic strength and originality that opened the door to international recognition. In 1950 he was selected for the Carnegie Prize, in 1952 for the Venice Biennale. In 1953 he won the Grand Prix at the São Paulo Biennale and exhibited at the Martha Jackson Gallery in New York. In Spain by this time the Francoist policy was to boost the most prominent names in Spanish abstract art, so as to give the regime a cultured, liberal image abroad. We should remember that, though Tàpies certainly showed his work in official exhibitions at that time, it would have been suicidal for any artist to confine himself to the international circuits (even if he had access to them) or to the meager artistic activities of the "opposition" to the regime. Regarding this point, as well as a detailed account of the contradictions, positions adopted and later contributions to the anti-Franco resistance, the artist's memoirs provide plenty of material.

The international context: non-figurative art, existentialism

Tàpies's work may be included in a European context presided over by what is called non-figurative painting and by the philosophical movement known as existentialism. Any detailed analysis of affinities and differences would take up far more space than is available to us here, but in general terms we might say that the men of that time formed a generation that had been led by the Second World War to reflect on the meaning of mankind and, in the field of art, to adopt similar plastic solutions. In this sense what Tàpies has in common with the existentialists is his interest in man as a subject and as a moral project, confronted with an infinite number of possibilities from which he must make his own choice. He also believes that man's existence is particular, historical and specific rather than a manifestation of any sort of absolute. One of the typical aspects of the existentialist vision is the belief that man's desire for self-knowledge is counterbalanced by negative aspects of existence, such as pain, frustration, sickness and death. According to Giulio Carlo Argan, Tàpies counters the radical ontologism of Heidegger (man is a being for death) with a "living with death." "He identifies with the object," says Argan, "albeit through a painful and always imperfect process of self-banishment...., filling the material with his own anguish.... What passes between these two poles is a turbulent stream of love and hate, pity and ferocity."

But Argan has likewise interpreted Tàpies's work, in relation to the historical and human context of his generation, as a metaphor not only of the darkness of Francoist Spain but also of other European "darknesses" of this century: fear, anxiety, prison, war. Such is the backdrop against which we must view non-figurative art, which emerged immediately after the Second World War. This art — also sometimes known as "matter" art — has been given positive or negative verdicts, depending on the critic dealing with it. According to Jean Cassou, for instance, it is simply a desperate denial of the world. Most of its defenders, however, speak of it as an art that lets matter express itself through itself. Many of them — especially when speaking of the works of Jean Fautrier — adduce as evidence the fact that the matter in question dissolves in an undefined chaos and talk of things being given plastic form at the very moment of their genesis, as though it were a question of some fundamental, original magma. Undoubtedly, the impulse of phenomenological philosophy in our century (Husserl, Merleau-Ponty), with the attention it pays to real experience and to things themselves, its non-distinction between being and seeming, has been an indirect influence for this poetry of textures, of the trivial (which in Samuel Beckett is transformed into the absurd) and the everyday. Non-figurative art has also been seen, however, as a reaction to the manifold alienations that deprive man of the possession of himself and as a condemnation of the false values of comfort and technological progress. In this respect the painter Jean Dubuffet could be compared to Tàpies, not only in his criticism of the Pharisaism and idealism of western culture, or his condemnation of anonymity and standardization, but also in the positive side of this repulsion, which consists of revaluing all that is most humble, most tangible — though Dubuffet, I should point out, can be distinguished from Tàpies in the bittersweet humor of his way of looking at things. There have been many readings of Tàpies' work, seen as nonfigurative art, which have denied it any iconographical dimension (in speaking of the dissolution of form in the material). They have enounced two typical interpretations derived from a mistaken view of the concept of matter as it applies to this painter: on the one hand we hear of it as a simple presentation of physical aspects in order to make direct sensorial experiments; on the other, vaguely philosophical connotations are adduced, in which the painted material would act as "original matter" in the face of human experience. For instance Tomás Llorens is the one who has best elucidated the difference between the philosophical term and what for Tàpies is a procedure: the mixing of powdered marble with latex or other materials, while other writers have felt tempted to absolutize the meaning of Tàpies' work. Michel Tapié, for instance, speaks of "pure painting" as a reaction to a present drowned in facile decorativism: "the dramatic content of his work.... does not owe anything to anecdote...., but to the act of painting in itself, the structure and the texture being the sole bearers of the whole of his ineluctable message." Juan Eduardo Cirlot, on the other hand, alluding to the spiritualization of matter — a feature that is quite evident in certain works by Tàpies — is led by quite the contrary route to say that "Tàpies knows that matter is the spirit...., which can be made manifest through structure and order." Thus a different plane such as that of art is subsumed in a philosophical statement of an idealistic kind: matter — the external reality — would have no existence of its own except as a projection of our reason or our psyche. In the art of this Catalan painter matter would be transformed into thought become object, a notion which comes quite close to Hegel's definition of art as the tangible expression of the Idea.

In rebutting certain critics who speak of nihilism or of a pessimistic reduction to the most sordid level of human life, Pere Gimferrer writes that in his opinion it is not a question of a mere ceremony of death but of a vestibule leading to the unknown: an art that brings on the advent of the sacred through its contemplative aspect and thus recovers a value that has been lost in our time. But Gimferrer goes even further, describing Tàpies as a metaphysical artist and his work as a vehicle for mystical contemplation which leads us to "rediscover communication with the spheres of the incommunicable, giving some meaning to the natural world." He also speaks of "redemption and salvation of the visible world, which can only be saved through the destruction of the mediating elements, in order that the flame of the essential may shine forth." In the dichotomy between the real and the divine, or between the profane and the sacred (for the ambiguity of the terms "the unknown" and "the incommunicable" is quite evident: it may also be the ultimate meaning of our existence, or a spiritual transcendence created by ourselves), Gimferrer seems to favor the second, as though objects, once purified, were to serve only as mediators in an experience which, in the case of mysticism, can only be lived through or, at most, evoked.

Gimferrer's phrase about "the flame of the essential" may even make us think of a certain Platonic idea; and we might be tempted to interpret it accordingly if we took some statements made by the painter himself quite literally: "If I sometimes draw a foot or a head, I immediately feel the need to destroy it, for it is not a real head but one inside which there is another that has to be discovered." Nothing could be closer to the concept of the archetype, the ideal model of a head that must be revealed by extracting the specificity of its representation. To my mind, however, in Tàpies' work there is nothing of the schematic or of withdrawal from reality, but rather an affirmation which is vital, passionate and even indiscriminate in presenting itself to us "warts and all," and which ennobles it through monumentalization. If he reduces and refines it, the process is an essentially poetic one: in this way his realism, far from being a mechanical or clumsily photographic vision of the world, becomes a truly essential realism. Taking reality as his starting point, he simplifies some things and magnifies others to give us an image that is at once stronger and more immediate. It is true that darkness, silence, solitude and emptiness heighten the mystical experience — or, at least, encourage a contemplative attitude, the content of which will depend on the ideas, experiences and beliefs of the viewer himself. But in any case the spirituality reverts, boomerang-fashion, in life, as the artist seems to hint in something he wrote in 1955: "Art is a sign, an object, something that suggests reality to us in our spirit." It may also be enlightening, perhaps, to indicate the genesis of his work and to quote some comments that have to do with the way in which not only the external world but also the emotions can be distilled into images. A passage he wrote in 1964 records his appreciation (so Leonardo-like and, therefore, so visual) of the details of the glazing on a teacup, which one must know how to discern and esteem; in 1967, there is the advice he gives to the readers of a children's magazine: "Look! Look right into things! And let yourselves be carried away by everything that echoes in your hearts what you see with your eyes...." And then there are his replies to Barbara Catoir, who interviewed him in 1982: "Every emotion gives me a sort of image, and I even make a note of each one on a piece of paper so as not to forget it.... This leads at once to a sort of struggle between the idea I want to express and the material form I give it...."

I will be returning to the subject of realism later; but for the moment I should like to go a little more deeply into the apparent dichotomy between negation and affirmation. Joan Teixidor, for instance, showing a very sensitive understanding of the world of Tàpies, believes that his work "tends to concealment," that it has something of a "voluntary desert" or an "obsessive silence" about it; but, he adds, in contrast to the emptiness there is always a certain faith that seems to be born of this same ascetic negation. In fact, as I have already suggested, part of the greatness of Tàpies' art is based on the monumental character it gives to all that is dark, that is to say to silence, death, flagellation. In its solemnity, in the effect of presence conveyed by its treatment, this theme escapes tenderness and shows signs of a sort of negative epic quality. Perhaps this is because, as Herbert Read said of Picasso's *Guernica*, an age like ours can produce only negative monuments. And in some cases, as we shall see in specific works, the marks of laceration are charged with an infinite pity.

In other cases, however, the tragic epic is contrasted (as that of Goya might be in his time) with a positive affirmation of the banal: everyday objects, uncontaminated by technological design — non-superfluos objects, their wear and tear evoking the hand of man and the services they have rendered to him. They are at the same time lay monuments to what is within our reach: a table, a chair, a stick, a blanket, a pair of spectacles. They imply both the intelligence of the man who created them and the long list of human actions carried out by their means: resting and making love, sheltering and reading, etc. The physiological and the intellectual are thus united without any sort of "class distinction," since for Tàpies — as for the eastern philosophers and, to some extent, the Dadaists of our own age — they are both manifestations of life. The eyeglasses, particularly, which help us to see better, or to see "more," are a kind of metaphor of art itself, of its capacity for making us see the reality that surrounds us through new eyes. Nobody will ever look in the same way at a peeling wall or a pile of straw, the folds of a blanket or the red rags tied to objects protruding from the back of a truck, after he has seen the works of Tàpies.

It might be stated — rightly from the sociological viewpoint but not from the aesthetic — that only a person who has enjoyed a fair standard of comfort can present or contemplate as artistic objects the humblest specimens from the repertory of objects in our everyday environment. It is well known that a poor person who suddenly becomes rich will often throw out his old furniture to make room for new pieces, which in most cases are not in good taste but simply bastard copies of "luxury" furniture or else of modern, functional models. Thus there is a gain in comfort — which is humanly just — but hardly in beauty. Against this it should be argued that the logic of everyday life does not apply to art. In the late 18th century Kant separated the notion of the useful from that of the beautiful; it was Burke, however, who in developing his category of the sublime established the fact that pain or terror, as long as they do not constitute a real threat to us, can be objects of aesthetic pleasure. For in the contemplation of art the functionality of an object (as distinct from that other functionality of art, which means the heightening of visual perception and its capacity for interpreting the world) is left in abeyance; a woodcutter does not see a forest in the same way as a botanist or an idle stroller who simply enjoys its beauty. Moreover, the consideration of "ignoble" objects as artistic motifs has had a rich tradition in history. Everyday objects appear in great profusion in Dutch painting, for instance, though it is true that they are always subordinate to an anecdote or to the picturesque. Zurbarán, on the other hand, invests them with a soberly monumental quality and a spiritual character very close to the poetics of Tàpies. In this regard we must agree with those who have established links, not so much of direct influence as of affinities in the results achieved, between the Catalan painter and certain literary-artistic works of the 17th-century Spanish school; I should perhaps add that in Tàpies' own collection there is a work attributed to Zurbarán. The works of Valdés Leal, Ribera and Caravaggio are likewise filled with such themes as pain, anguish and death; and they are a constant leitmotiv in the world of the Romantics and in all the various expressionist schools.

A many-faceted realism

I have spoken of possible meanings in Tàpies' work and of the importance of objects — which has also been a constant in all forms of realist art. But how is this affirmation of realism to be interpreted? In a very broad sense undoubtedly, as being articulated in accordance with two basic ideas, one of which is that of representation and the other that of the importance of the theme, of the icon. That is why Hans Platschek is so right when he says that "Tàpies shows us that the picture is, above all, a visual fact. But it is not only that: [his pictures] give evidence of a theme...." Thus, the relevance of what we see (or what we endeavour to recognize), or the importance of the sign, contradicts that interpretation of Tàpies' art which was based on non-figurative criteria and in which it was presupposed that form dissolved into texture. Tàpies himself once remarked to Cirici Pellicer that the materials Dubuffet and Fautrier were using in the fifties seemed vague and ill-defined, like chocolate, whereas he himself preferred to choose materials that said something in themselves (any material, in fact, is charged with connotations, but it is the will to say something and the differences between definition and non-definition that interest us here).

It has been a fairly frequent practice with certain critics to attribute a realist character to Tàpies's work; such critics, however, usually allude to one form or another, one or other of the resources of representation used by the painter. Cirici, for instance, based his argument for realism on the material as a procedure, especially on the transition from oil paint to a thicker pigment and from "magical" illusion to collage. Herbert Read was of the opinion that these works "are not naturalistic, but neither are they non-figurative or convulsed," which suggests the problem clearly but only with reference to the presentation: "it is simply a physical object, with no other magic than that created before our eyes by the wind and the rain." And Giulio Carlo Argan was to say, more profoundly, that this painting "maintains its condition as an object, not in the sense of representation but in that of an ineluctable precipitation and reification of this representation." Thus, one of them (Cirici) speaks of denser or more real materials; another (Read) of a presentation, or possibly a paraphrase, of nature; and the third (Argan), finally, of a representation that becomes an object. For the fact is that Tàpies' art is not only voluntarily ambiguous — a condition of all poetry — but also extremely complex in its relationship to reality and its ways of representing it or, if you like, giving it to us in a work. In general terms we should speak of different procedures, among which are the *apparently illusionistic representation of the textures*, the *transposition of textures*, the *presentation of real objects* and those devices which allude to reality, or to its memory, such as *footprints* and *fingerprints, graphic signs* or *mnemonic images*. We should also mention the fact that, when we consider his work as a whole, we find both an effect of presence and an elusion, both totality and fragmentation or "piecing." If we wish to understand this sort of device better and so avoid generalizations that always run the risk of being mistaken, our best plan is to analyze and examine the works themselves. Before approaching this task, however, there is one point that should be made clear: the comments below are not arranged chronologically, for the simple reason that since the Surrealist works of the *Dau al Set* period there have been no great breaks with the past or stylistic changes in Tàpies' painting. The themes are constant and the procedures recurrent, with occasional innovations such as, for instance, that of the objects in the seventies (with the precedent of *Metal Shutter and Violin* in 1956) or the greater degree of illusionism in the eighties — which, however, do not necessarily entail the abandonment of other methods.

Moreover, though based on a distinction between different ways of representing, the possible meanings of each theme are of the utmost importance, as is any possible comparison with other works of direct or indirect influence. Regarding this latter point, it is not a question of establishing who was the first artist to achieve a "formal advance" or a particular invention (though this might well constitute the subject of a specialized study elsewhere); it is obvious that there is a constant interrelationship between images and artists, and that there is a steadily growing tendency to appraise the strength and quality of a painter's *œuvre* independently of the spectacular breaks with the past made by some of the avant-garde artists of our century.

In the case of Tàpies it is very important to point out that he has generally been studied by writers belonging to a more strictly literary field, and that an analysis establishing purely artistic comparisons, together with a close study of certain specific works, was therefore clearly needed.

Imitation through textures

The 19th-century French realist painter Gustave Courbet was highly criticized in his time for representing principally the texture of an object — its "skin," as it were. For this artist emphasized the physical appearance of objects, their smooths and their roughs, their transparency and their gloss, and since he thus dealt with aspects considered hardly noble enough for painting, he was censured by his contemporaries for vulgarity and coarseness — reminiscent of the criticism levelled at Tàpies by some Catalan art lovers of today. Manuela Mena mentions, as another precedent for non-figurative painting (in the equation between material used and matter represented), Goya's celebrated *Dog* (today in the Prado) apparently crouching in sand, because of the thickness of its pigment, which simulates to perfection the earthy qualities of its subject (though it is still not certain whether this characteristic may not be the result of the mural having been moved).

If we look today at a work like *White with Red Stains* (Fig. 9), which Tàpies painted in 1954, its texture will at once lead us to associate it with a wall inscribed with street graffiti. The illusionism is not complete, however, for the painter has placed this whitish material on a surface covered with varnish — which, incidentally, prefigures the plentiful use of varnish in his more recent works. The theme of the wall is highly charged with references; it comes from memories both of the old walls in the Gothic Quarter and of the Spanish Civil War. They are spaces for contemplating the passage of time, a kind of modern *Vanitas*, and at the same time, with their worn, shabby, almost dishonored appearance, a sort of metaphor of the history of man himself, his hopes and dreams, the punishments inflicted on him. It was also at this time, as José L. Barrio-Garay reminds us, that Tàpies, after reading Bodhidharma's *Contemplation of the Wall in Mahayana*, recognized the similarities between Zen contemplation and contemplation of the wall, which acts as a support or medium leading to other thoughts. Undoubtedly, both Leonardo's advice to the young to gaze at the stains on a wall, full of evocations, and the romantic theme of ruins (a veritable archaeology of tragedy), which has been interpreted as a symbol of protest against the positivism of the modern age, are remote ancestors of this predilection for walls. We should also remember the photographs of Atget and Brassai in the 1920s, on the old walls of Paris (Brassai's importance is recognized by Tàpies himself in his famous text *Communication on the Wall*).

Returning to *White with Red Stains*, in its center we see a roughly scratched circle, three lines like fingerprints, an X-shaped cross, another circle in paint and two stains. As Tomás Llorens has pointed out, what separates these signs from symbols and emblems is their unconventional character, the impossibility of deciphering them according to a finite code decided upon beforehand by custom or tradition. The artist himself has said that he places certain signs in his works because he likes them, and in this we should perhaps see both their purely plastic function within the composition as a whole and a subconscious reaction (the A or the T for the initials of his name, for instance, or the X-shaped cross as a sign of erasure and, therefore, of rejection and breaking-off). But neither is there anything to prevent us from reading them differently, as when Barbara Catoir reminds us that an X is the signature of an illiterate or that a V can be the symbol of a funeral.

The X stands out clearly in white on the "wall" of the 1955 *Large Gray Painting* (Fig. 12). When some authors speak about the representation becoming an object, they are really alluding to the fact that the picture loses its illusory quality and turns into another independent reality. But since it is obvious that no picture, however illusionistic, can be reality itself, this objectification in Tàpies is heightened not only by the physical materials employed, which imitate textures, but also by an emphasis on bas-relief and by the enclosure of the forms that we find in some of his works. In *Large Gray Painting* the material that makes one think of a peeling wall is in fact arranged far from fortuitously: in a great central mass, the lower edge of which makes a shape that will appear frequently in other works, such as *Material in the Shape of a Nut* (Fig. 29) or, more schematically, *"Et amicorum"* (Fig. 57). This organic form provides a break in what would otherwise be excessively geometrical and makes the mass susceptible to a possible anthropomorphic reading, with a suggestion of buttocks and female pudenda (or an anal orifice) that was to be more pronounced in other pictures. This form, in short, prevents the work from being seen as the mere texture of a wall, though it might of course be a fragment of it (and yet arranged like that by the artist). We should remember, moreover, that the fragmented vision is a typical feature of the modern perception (though with occasional forerunners among the Mannerists, for instance), appearing profusely in the works of Degas and the Impressionists. But Tàpies makes only partial use of this device; what prevails here is the composition and an intricate interplay of balances and ambiguities which show us, above all, the figure (in its broadest sense, not just a human figure); one has the sensation that, if the central rectangle continued in the upper part (notice, too, the "entrance" in the upper left-hand corner), the picture would be a failure. Something similar occurs with Mondrian, whose concern to break up strict mathematical symmetry nevertheless produces a work possessing a new equilibrium.

In *Hieroglyphics* (Fig. 14), done between 1958 and 1960, the surface covered by graffiti-like scrawls seems to be cut off haphazardly on the left, but it contrasts with a blue background and the lines of its writing initiate a falling movement towards the right; the wall has become a kind of cliff because the different blues remind us of water and the sky. Again and again culture, though in this case in the form of an indecipherable code, is united with nature. Tàpies' fascination with archaeology, moreover, dates back a long time, to those schooldays when the subject he chose for an essay was *The Kingdom of Ur and Cuneiform Script*. Besides, traces of the past are not only highly evocative (as Tàpies himself has said of ruins and objects worn by the passage of time), but at the same time provide a further allusion to all that is secret, recondite or incommunicable in the case of hieroglyphics. The hieroglyphics arouse our interest, not only because our reason has been incapable of revealing their meaning but also — as it proved for the Surrealists, who were fond of such indecipherable writings — because it represents certain symbolic coordinates that differ from those of western culture.

There are some works in which the form and the texture might at first sight seem to be almost a kind of *trompe l'œil*. *Material in the Shape of a Nut* (Fig. 29), for instance, certainly seems to imitate the wrinkled outer integument of a walnut. If we examine it carefully, however, we will see that this work is by no means hyperrealist, since it does not exactly represent either the outer surface of the nutshell or its interior, or even the walnut itself. The natural curve of the nutshell (which in a traditional representation would be shown by shading) has been flattened in this case basically by means of a central slash and a groove or striation near the bottom parallel to the edge of the canvas. The considerable dimensions (195 × 175 cm) of the painting enlarge it monstrously, transforming this nut above all into a surface that is closer to the wrinkles of an old human skin (Cirici, for instance, saw the pudenda of an old woman in this work). However, we cannot escape the *gestalt* of the walnut, not only on account of the title but also because of the outline against a monochrome background. This exaggerated enlargement of an object, as though seen in a close-up, had appeared in works by Magritte like the 1953 *Chambre d'écoute* or the 1960 *Tombeau des lutteurs*, in which an enormous apple and a rose, respectively, are enclosed in rooms (but in Magritte, of course, there is a high degree of illusionism), as it was also to appear in the work of several Pop artists painting at the same time as Tàpies produced this picture. We might recall, too, the half-open walnut traversed by an arrow in Max Ernst's famous picture entitled *Oedipus Rex* (1922), in which the walnut (like the hand and the birds) is similarly disproportionate to the house. In dealing with this type of composition in an enclosed oval, however, we should also remember (given Tàpies' interest in eastern art and thought) certain mandalas, as well as the Jainist maps, in which a circle or a flattened oval is placed in a square or rectangular frame, whether touching the sides or not.

In those maps and mandalas the oval or circular form represents the universe with all its elements; and we generally tend to associate the oval form with the idea of genesis (cells, embryos, etc.) or with that of the birth of the world (the very title, for instance, of a work by Brancusi that consists of a white marble egg, and also suggested in *The World Egg* by Mark Tobey, done in 1944). This association is more evident in Tàpies' 1957 *White Oval* (Fig. 15), albeit by means of a paradox: on the one hand its whiteness removes it from connotations of materials, bringing it close to an almost metaphysical light like that of Malevich's *White on White* (1920), while on the other it presents this crackled surface, like an elephant's hide or the surface of dry, burnt earth. We might also bear in mind that oval form subsists, in the subconscious of any painter, as that of a traditional format in the history of painting, one which first appeared in the 17th century but certainly continued in the framing of much later works of a type still frequently to be found in certain bourgeois interiors (hence its parodying by the Cubists, for instance). But even in our western tradition these forms are susceptible to a cosmological interpretation; thus, the ball held in his hand by the Child Jesus in medieval carvings is a symbol of the universe.

But this similarity of forms (since *White Oval* is a notably ambiguous work) has led me momentarily to forget the textures that seemed to imitate real textures. An ultimate example of this can be found in the 1968 work *Material in the Shape of an Armpit* (Fig. 28), in which the illusionism seems perfect: the hair is real, the red gashes perfect simulations of wounds. Here, however, the painter has not enlarged a small object but has cut a fragment of a body, which may explain why Miró (who owned the work) once told Georges Raillard that he could not see any armpit in it. But apart from that, and although the material provides what is almost a bas-relief, in this work we find none of the concern for anatomy (basically, the care taken to indicate the musculature accurately), and the area between the shoulder and the neck is prolonged excessively.

Transposition of textures

A procedure rather different from the "illusionism" of textures is that of their transposition, by which I mean using the qualities of one surface for another which really possesses different qualities. In this way the poetic force of an object is increased by means of an operation of metonymy or metaphor.

Thus Courbet, for instance, painted the sea with an earthen color and consistency, or a woman bathing whose thigh takes on the qualities of the rock she is leaning against, while Picasso painted his *Three Women* (1908-1909) as though they were carved out of the very mountain, with flesh resembling wood or earth, and volumes and planes that seem to have been produced by strokes of an axe. It is with a more schematic approach that Tàpies presents, in 1959, his *Form of a Crucified Figure* (Fig. 19), in which the body acquires the same consistency as the background: that of a thick wall with a uniform dark brown color. However — and not only on the score of the title — the outspread arms, the outline of the torso and the clearly-marked chest and navel compel us to see it as a human fugure. Its head is no more than a rectangle with ochers and whites; the holes may be seen as the traces of the crown of thorns; the blood from the wounds has spread to the horizontal band that seems to bear the physical weight of pain; the figure's immobility and stiffness are reminiscent of Romanesque carvings.

In a 1973 painting, *Earth and Blue* (Fig. 44), the title may speak of earth but the form suggests an outline brutally cut and finished off by a sky blue. The graceful, sand-colored lines on the right give life to what is virtually a buttock and are prolonged in an upward-escaping movement (we might almost imagine a kind of earthen and even more mutilated *Victory of Samothrace*). "B, solitude" and "A, desert," written on the right-hand side, are taken from a poem by Joan Brossa; they are perhaps meant to express the non-communication of childhood, which in any case may lead to adult solitude. Here too, however, we find a typical transposition of elements from the ancient cosmogonies, contrasting earth as the origin of man (Genesis, the Babylonian myths) with the watery element as a spiritual symbol and the source of life.

Objects

A logical solution to this concern for reality felt by Tàpies is the presentation of objects just as they are. This may be an extension, not only of certain spaces blocked in their dense materiality, which are given the character of bas-reliefs by the mixture of powdered marble and latex, but also of the works done in 1945 and 1946 in which the painter had used real elements (newsprint, threads, textiles) — and some of which were presented, really, as objects (like the *Box of Strings*, which could be viewed from both sides). Around the beginning of the sixties this objectification was accentuated by the inclusion of cardboard (*Cardboard and String*, 1959), ropes (*Ropes Crossing on Wood*, 1960), canvas (*Crossed Canvas*, 1962) and even a comb (*Collage of Comb on Cardboard*, 1961). Other pictures are already objects independent of any background or support, like the stretchers presented in 1962 (which bore painted signs or paint) or the 1960 *Paint on Wood*, a sort of wooden trunk or chest painted on both sides (like a "reversible" medallion, according to V. Linhartová). Towards the end of the sixties these object-pictures (or the objects themselves) became more frequent, coinciding with the emergence of *Arte povera* in Italy.

The inclusion of real materials in works of art has by now become a tradition in our century (e). Paper appeared with the Cubists as a plastic element of color or as an indication of the texture of an object, though in some Cubist works we also find real objects. The Russian Constructivists, too, used wood, iron and paper as elements more "real" than pigment; and Tàpies himself is quite prepared to recognize (rightly) the impact on his work of Gaudí's use of pottery shards. But it was most particularly Marcel Duchamp who, with his ready-mades, opened up an

(e) Miró: *Wind Clock*, 1967.

22

(f) Barry Flanagan: *Untitled*, 1967.

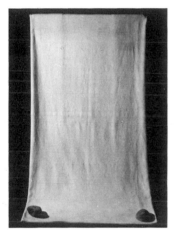

(g) Tàpies: *Blanket with Two Stones*, 1971.

immense field of possibilities for contemporary art. His objects, always prefabricated or mass-produced (a bottle rack, a urinal, a snow shovel), selected by the artist and decontextualized, now acquired a possible aesthetic dimension. Duchamp's breakthrough, so to speak, was a gesture more than anything else, but it did confirm the principle that art is not a fiction but, above all else, a selective gaze. His innovation was reflected in Dada and Surrealist objects, though in these the everyday object was filled with humor or mystery.

Tàpies' objects do not possess the impersonality aimed at by Duchamp, nor are they a provocative challenge to the art community (though they may well be one for the more general public). They are absolutely a part of his personal poetics, contained within the framework of certain objectives which the artist himself has stated explicitly in speaking of his work as a whole: "To remind man of what he really is; to provide him with a theme for meditation; to cause him a shock that will awaken him from the frenzy of the unauthentic, so that he may discover himself and become conscious of his real possibilities; these are the goals my art endeavours to reach." They are, then, vehicles for meditation, which is something very different from the positivism of the Italian *Arte povera* artists. For these painters, to quote their apologist, Germano Celant, "the artist does not re-process the material with which he comes into contact; he passes no judgment, seeks no moral, social values; he does not manipulate (the material) but leaves it to appear, uncovered, awaiting the arrival of the natural phenomenon, like the growth of a plant, the chemical reaction of a mineral...." Today, over ten years later, this declaration of strict empirical neutrality does not seem applicable to all the works of *Arte povera*: in some, for instance, the virtual component was very strong, and on the whole they may be read today not only as a gesture (a Utopian one, of course) against the art market but also as a reaction to an excessively technological world. But it is true that, compared with the rubbish heaps or clothing piles of the Italian artists, whose experience seems to be the result of chance (f), Tàpies' works seem "composed," some of them — like the 1970 *Covered Chair* or the 1971 *Blanket with Two Stones* (g) — invested with a secret elegance, which led V. Linhartová to say that there is "an immutable presence of things."

If we look, however, we will see that no object ever appears alone (even a pile of plates is an accumulation, and when there are forty-four of them they form a column, a monument to the everyday); the association of ideas is basic, as in all his works. Thus, for instance, a pile of newspapers is placed on a basin, the two things united by their shared "cast-off" character, or associating reading and illness, everyday history and the physiological; a wicker basket — an example of well-finished craftsmanship — is surrounded by an untidy tangle of wire: this "barrier" against anyone's picking it up makes us see it differently (as something which is caught, but also as a sculpture).

Except for the 1971 work *Mirror and Collage* (Fig. 39) and *Piece of Cloth* (Fig. 45), done in 1973 (which in any case have to lean against, or hang from, a wall), the objects reproduced in this book are not freestanding but may all be described, roughly, as rectangular objects attached to a wall and thus still sharing the connotation of the "picture" format. Or, better still, they convert a banal material or object into a picture — i.e., into culture — *by means of a displacement*. In the same way as Rauschenberg hung his own bed from the (paint-spattered) wall, so Tàpies in turn uses a material that is heaped up, straw (*Straw and Wood*, Fig. 31), sticking it on to the canvas and letting it cascade down over the surface, like a head of hair (the lath crossing it exactly halfway is essential to the balance of the composition, giving order and symmetry to the undulating tangle). The straw he used very often in 1968 and 1969 is covered with blankets or, as in *Large Parcel of Straw* (Fig. 38), with white paper. The persistence with which Tàpies includes vertical rectangular shapes and the profusion in his work of shapes recalling that of a bed make us see this parcel covered by a piece of crumpled paper as a pillow on a bed. Straw, moreover, is at once warm and rough, like the texture of dreams.

The 1970 painting *Blue and Sack* (Fig. 36) also suggests a bed, this time by wrapping the blue-paper-covered canvas in a sack. As in *Straw and Wood* (Fig. 31), here an object whose "natural" position would be on the floor is placed vertically. Leo Steinberg has rightly pointed out that western painting, down to and including Pollock, represents a space (abstract or concrete) corresponding to the erect human figure, with the upper edge at the height of a man's head and the lower one lying more or less where we put our feet. Steinberg detects a break with this principle (prefigured by Monet's *Water Lilies* and Mondrian's "crosses," etc.) in certain works by Dubuffet and Rauschenberg, in which this verticality is cancelled out. It is the transition, Steinberg rather exaggeratedly tells us, from nature (or from the visual act) to culture. To me this line of thought suggests that when Tàpies places his banal objects in an arrangement accentuating the verticality that characterizes both the format of western painting and man himself, he is using this device to elevate or ennoble materials that are at ground level and human actions likewise associated with our most instinctive or physiological nature, such as sleeping, lying in bed after illness or procreating. Here, therefore, a "classic" arrangement is used for a change of content. As for the procedure, it is interesting to observe that because of the heaviness of the material the vast majority of these works are painted on the ground and afterwards placed on walls.

One of the best examples of empathy between the "nobility" of culture and the coarsest, earthiest aspects of life is the inclusion, as a theme, of excrement, bloodstains or detritus. In *Black and Earth* (Fig. 34), painted in 1970, the same brown ("like that of dung," says the painter) is given to the paint on the canvas and the earth and straw at the bottom. Not only is the painting thus naturally prolonged in the material, but there is also a wooden support that joins the two things. At the top we are shown the dimensions of the work in centimeters, its direction (with arrow) and the date of its execution, with all the coldness of a catalogue entry. And although this may be an echo of the conceptual artist's empirical passion for measurements, it is also true that its significance here is much more complex: it recalls the artistic metalanguage inherent in any work of art and at the same time its material, temporal condition as a cultural product — which blends, however, with the earth itself or with the humblest of castoffs, thus showing its "sacralization" by the marked (or by scholars), together with an evident "desacralization."

Finally, *Piece of Cloth* (Fig. 45) can also be included in a whole series of works using different kinds of cloth, which may be glued to the canvas, used to cover objects or almost freestanding, like this one. The cloths are folded, creased, tied in knots, stuffed; they may hide or partially cover objects; seldom has such humble material — for they are usually shabby blankets or sheets, or coarse kitchen cloths — been worked to such evocative advantage. Sometimes they paraphrase man and his feelings, as when a bulky, stuffed piece of cloth resembles a potbelly, or when a knotted cloth recalls a tramp's bundle and at the same time the complicated knotting of our own passions, ideas or unresolved problems. But these cloths are also part of the long tradition of drapery in western art (i), and Tàpies passes from the evocation of the Holy Shroud to the elegant fall of the cloth in the 1970 work *Covered Chair* (h), or actually subverts this fall by folding the piece as a salesman would in *Piece of Cloth* (and yet the folded part again suggests the form of a cushion, hanging from a wire if not by a thread).

A final use of cloths, and one that is specifically linked to the classical tradition, is that of effects. Recalling the procedure of the ancients, who used to wet draperies in order to bring out even more clearly the forms of the human body, Tàpies places an object under a wet cloth so as to mark its outline and volume, which he then fixes with an airbrush. *Effect of Stick in Relief* (Fig. 58) and *Effect of Body in Relief* (Fig. 60), both done in 1979, are examples of this procedure. Here the painter has used a very old method indeed, and one that was of great importance in academic training, but he has given it a slightly different significance. In Ancient Greece draperies could be used either for decorative purposes (with the still rather schematic folds of the archaic period) or to enhance the forms of the body and endow the figure with movement, turning to account at the same time the plastic possibilities in the movements of the cloth, the latter being seen as something artificial with a life of its own. For Tàpies, however, this is an extension of the human trace, the mark left by the body: a theme that appears with profusion in his work, as an evocation, an impression charged with mystery, a memory. It is also associated with several of his works in which an object is covered or concealed, such as the sacks, the parcels, the bundles, the stretchers covered

(h) Tàpies: *Covered Chair,* 1970.

(i) *Koré,* c. 470-450 B. C.

with cloth, etc. In contrast, then, to the straightforward presentation of an armpit, here we have evocation through shadows or through impressions left on the sand or on a wall — a setting-up of barriers, as it were, in order thus to sharpen the viewer's imagination. In the covering-up process he re-created the mysteriousness of Man Ray's famous photograph, *The Enigma of Isidore Ducasse* (1920). There may also be an echo of Brossa's fascination with magic, which questions the real appearance of things and may in turn be applied to art, the ambiguity of which can suggest many meanings; as there is likewise a suggestion of eastern philosophy, especially in its notion of *maya*, the illusion that presents itself as the world of phenomena. More than one writer has suggested that in this urge to conceal there is a desire to insinuate the ultimate meaning of things; the *Effect of Body in Relief* may indeed suggest to some viewers the Platonic shadow of the myth of the cavern which in this case would be concealing the essence of the idea of a body. But the outline, for all its elusiveness, presents a specific materiality that is in no way idealized: the open legs and the contorted hands, like those of a skeleton, suggest a specific sensation of pain, oppression and claustrophobia under the sheets.

Ambiguous perspectives, poetic geometries, empty spaces

We have been reminded on numerous occasions that *The Legerdemain of Wotan*, painted in 1950, marks the first time that a bed appears in Tàpies' work. In this case, with a sharpening of the feeling of a dream atmosphere, the bed was considerably elongated and its perspective distorted, while the profusion of blankets and bulky shapes made its spatial orientation imprecise. Later on the theme of the bed was to appear frequently in his paintings, giving rise to further distortions of conventional perspective. Apart from this, however, a bed (like a chair or a ladder) has a geometrical structure, and this geometry is a fundamental feature in the painter's work as a framework for his compositions, a redoubt of classicism and a factor of orderliness that contrasts with the fleshy quality of the material or with organic forms. For Tàpies, moreover, the bed holds memories of an adolescence plagued by illness, as well as being the support for man's physiological or instinctive aspects.

One of the most impressively sober of these beds is the 1960 *Brown Bed* (Fig. 22), which the painter himself affectionately calls "the bed of St Francis." There is no suggestion of cast-offs about the homogeneous brown here; indeed, its glazing and the way the light touches the wrinkles on the pillow give it a sort of splendor of its own, as of immanent spirituality. But the ties to earth and the human condition of the preacher of poverty are marked by the two hollows at the level of the feet — like the saint's stigmata — and by the "imprint" of his head on the pillow. The bed is seen from overhead, though we are given a frontal view of two of its feet, as in some children's or primitive drawings, except that here they are like an anthropomorphic prolongation of the bed itself. This alteration of the perspective comes, ultimately, from the lesson of Cubism, particularly analytical Cubism, in which the forms are simplified and a surface perpendicular to the plane of the canvas may be shown as parallel to it — as we see, for instance, in Picasso's *The Artist's Dining-Room, Rue de la Boëtie*, painted in 1919 (j).

The 1963 work entitled *Large Material with Side Papers* (Fig. 24), though apparently a wall, may also be seen as a bed if we follow this scheme of flatness I have just described. But Tàpies curbs any possible illusionism by means of the papers stuck to the edges, thus accentuating the picture's character as a finite, enclosed object. This tension at the edges is found in quite a few other works, such as *Gray Corners on Brown* (1959), *Four Holes* (1960), *Ocher with Six Collages* (1963), *Slate* (1965), *Ocher with Six Incisions* (1964) or the 1978 work *Oval 1-2* (Fig. 56), and it represents in fact an extension of the problems concerning the format and limit of the canvas which were worked out by certain American abstract artists. This emphasizing of the border areas means a break with the importance formerly conceded to the central motif, though in *Large Material* — as in other works by

(j) Picasso: *The Artist's Dining-Room, Rue de la Boëtie*, 1919.

Tàpies — our perception is ambivalent: our gaze is forced towards the center, but we can not forget the presence of these margins.

The rectangular shape so omnipresent in Tàpies contrasts with the square shape which may be that of the format or that of squares formed by subdivisions of a rectangular space, like the ones we see in transpositions from one drawing to another, larger one or to a different support. A kind of geometrical network (virtual and denied, as in *Large Material*, or explicit, as in other works) appears quite frequently and makes one think of works in which, though they are different in appearance, share the importance of geometry as the arranger of the space: in the work of Rothko, Ad Reinhardt and Ellsworth Kelly, for example.

As for the square, it is a static, severe and rational shape; in symbology it is usually associated with the ordering of four elements, such as the points of the compass, the seasons or the elements of earth, air, water and fire. A possible religious origin might be found in the temple, which at first meant a square, circumscribed space for protecting the sacred element (*contemplare*, incidentally, derives from *templum*). In its strict symmetry it is regarded as an ordered, perfect form, and Tàpies conceals it by covering a square stretcher with a larger square of cloth, in the 1976 painting *Square on Square* (Fig. 53), indicating the corners with strokes of black. In *Oval 1-2* (Fig. 56), painted in 1978, the strict angularity is broken by the wads of paper wrapping the four corners; thus, as in certain works in which the frame accentuates the painted forms it encloses (for example, in Joan Miró's 1943 *Painting with Art-Nouveau Frame*, or when the format establishes a relationship with what is painted (as in Raphael's celebrated *Madonna della Sedia*), here the four rounded corners continue the curve of the central oval, which can be read as the letter O, as a plate or tray, or as the schematized form of a mirror. All concentrically arranged figures, all radial or spherical arrangements and all circles or squares with central points may be ascribed to the symbolism of the mandalas, as Frieda Fordham tells us in her introduction to Jung's *Psychology*, and thus act as media for contemplation or for the purpose of adoration. Obviously there is more ambiguity in any modern work of art, but we should not forget the survival in Tàpies' style of the formal archetypes which are frequently found in eastern, primitive or ornamental art, as possible points of reference.

The wardrobe and door motif, which is also frequent, not only evokes memories but indicates the duality between the inner and the outer world or, sometimes, the impossibility of attaining the occult or the struggle to do so. There is a certain tendency to show closed doors, blocked or partially covered spaces, as in *Wardrobe Door* (Fig. 46), which even appears sealed with the painter's monogram (AT), used also as his signature to the work. In the 1978 *"Et amicorum"* (Fig. 57) only the pointed shapes of the friends' shoes stand out in the dark, concentrated structure. But this motif of confinement is countered by the empty, ethereal spaces, equally enigmatic but somewhat more restful color. The 1969 *Large Door* (Fig. 30), in a lighter, sand-colored material, has the contrasting note of a white in the middle which is almost that of the supernatural light of a Gothic lancet window. It is a doorway of initiation, inducing thoughts of threshold crossing, penetration and entrance into an unknown beyond.

The Ladder (Fig. 49), painted in 1974, also suggests a metaphor of ascension, and therefore of elevation, but its ambiguous perspective (as though seen upside down) and the way it contrasts with furrow that twists and turns in the material above it refer us to a horizontal plane likewise placed vertically *a posteriori*. It recalls that phrase of Lin Yutang which tells us that we must learn to live "crawling over the earth and the sand, being happy," without any need for supernatural worlds, knowing that Heaven is in ourselves.

The void has been a constant motivation in Tàpies' work and thought, being as it is not only a characteristic feature of certain works in his favorite forms of art (eastern, medieval and archaic art, as opposed to Baroque, which he cannot stand) but also a recurrent theme in the philosophy of Heidegger, Sartre and eastern mysticism and wisdom. This last is governed by the suspension of contradictions (which is not the same as a dialectic of harmony), in contradistinction to the notion of accumulation and competitiveness in western knowledge. A certain primitivism in the one contrasts with the notion of strife and "might is right" in

the other; the disappearance of the ego, innocence and effortless action are thus confronted with subjectivism and aggressiveness. Though eastern thought is, in effect, an alternative to ours, it nevertheless possesses a fairly large proportion of immobilism, which assorts badly with other characteristic features of Tàpies' thinking and working methods: not only the destructive force of the tearings and incisions in some of his works, but also his desire for shock and effects on reality, which is an echo of the avant-garde movement and perhaps, too, a consequence of the ideology of Marxism, a system that aspires to change the world and, in this case, the way in which that world should be seen.

The void, in short, may be proposed as an authentic affirmation, as in the case of the 1974 work entitled *Sí* (Fig. 50), as solitary as a graffito in the middle of a wall, though accentuated by two lines drawn with a ruler (it might be compared, perhaps, with the famous *No* by Jasper Johns (k), though the latter is more "suffering" with its blobs of dripping paint). And the painter, in speaking about the void, also tells us of "a strange nostalgia, almost always linked to — and denouncing — the feeling of separation that brings us face to face with what we really are." As in Kant's moral reflection on the sublime, the immensity of nature arouses a two-way feeling: the human sensation of physical helplessness in the face of nature and the later exaltation of the forces of the soul, which gives us our measure and our superiority to nature. In Tàpies, however, the consciousness of this rending is aimed at a new harmony between man and the natural world.

Bodies

The human figure appeared frequently in the works done between 1944 and 1951, in primitive, schematic or demoniacal form. The two realistically drawn profiles in the 1953 *Ox Cart* are in vivid contrast to *The Inner Fire*, painted in the same year, in which a torso is represented simply by a piece of sacking eroded by burns. In 1956 we find a *Landscape-Figure* (Fig. 16) drawn on a reddish background and extremely ambivalent: in view of other, later works it may be seen as a forerunner of the female figures with fallen breasts (as exaggerated here as in any prehistoric "Venus"), or else as a kneeling figure with swollen thighs. The head cut off at the neck and the inscriptions like cracks all over the body will appear again in other works; the rectangle containing the figure, itself placed on a surface like that of a weatherbeaten wall, makes one think of a poster.

When a body (or part of a body) appears in Tàpies' work, it is usually shown wounded, lacerated or covered with marks, as though revealing the physical pain or aggression it has suffered. To produce this effect the painter uses incisions, scrawls and erasures, or he may present the bodies in postures proper to victims or simply degrading: kneeling, with legs open, etc. It is as though the body were the object most prone to destruction, to the ineluctable fate of a sadistic impulse, an extension — as the psychoanalysts would say — of the death impulse. In *Ocher and Pink Relief* (Fig. 25), for instance, we see a woman's body, kneeling and clinging to the end or side of some piece of furniture, perhaps a bed. Her sunken breasts appear again in *Body of Material and Orange-Colored Stains* (Fig. 33), in which the decrepitude is like that in Van Gogh's drawing, *Affliction* (l). But in *Body of Material* there is also a reddish-brown stain, evoking menstruation or excrement, and the whole of this headless figure is enclosed in an oval, as though metaphorically alluding to fecundation. This destructive impulse and these scatological or afflictive themes can be read in many different ways: on the one hand there is the desire to "degrade" the classical idealization of the naked human figure (as there is in the alteration of the classical order in more abstract compositions covered with scrawls or erasures), and likewise to break with an excessive realism; on the other, each of these works can be interpreted as a sort of lay *Vanitas*, as though saying: "We are this too, make no mistake about it. Finally, by virtue of the current of empathy to be found in the expressionist styles, there may be a feeling of commiseration for the physical state described, a kind of infinite pity that makes these

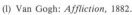

works Votive offerings. As with suffering and fear in Greek tragedy (which is itself so sanguinary incidentally), the viewer of these works may be led to meditate on the human condition, no longer seeing it as something bound to the workings of a *fatum*, but perhaps knowing how to accept that fundamental cruelty which Antonin Artaud speaks of as being essential to the awakening of man: "[The theater]," says Artaud, "rediscovers the notion of figures and archetypes, which function as sudden moments of silence, pauses, intermittent heartbeats, stimulation of the lymph, inflammatory images that invade the suddenly awakened mind..., disturbing the repose of the senses, liberating the repressed subconscious, encouraging a virtual rebellion...."

The human presence may likewise appear indirectly, as occurs in the case of the two arcs in *All White with Arcs* (Fig. 20), suggesting the pectoral curves of a hypothetical, empty torso. Or it may do so metaphorically, returning to formal archetypes like those that constrast female/organic forms with male/geometric forms, as in *White and Ocher on Brown* (Fig. 21). The body may take its condition of animality as an example of the more extended notion of objects, in a work whose title alludes to the core of the basic problem in the act of knowing or grasping reality: *Subject-Object* (Fig. 61), painted in 1979, which contrasts a scrawled foot with the prolongation of a cross that becomes an arm or a kneeling leg, on which the black lines are those of an archaic or animal hairiness.

Finally, linking up with the theme of signs and allusions, many corporal presences make their appearance through trace-prints, as in *Sardana-Circle of Feet* (Fig. 43), or through a kind of *sfumato*, as in that *Back* (Fig. 69) which is glimpsed through shadows and seems to emerge from space with a perspective reminiscent of Renaissance exercises (the disproportion of the body, moreover, makes one think of Goya's *Colossus*, here tinged with lyricism and a sense of classical order).

Elusive presences

Though constantly using different techniques while remaining faithful to his motifs, in recent years Tàpies seems to be showing a certain preference for an extension of the imprint theme. Thus we see the "out-of-focus" presences, the shadows or the representations of things with varnish bringing back the idea of evocation, reflection or echo and breaking up (as Leonardo's *sfumato* did) the Renaissance clarity or the accumulation of matter in earlier works. Cirici Pellicer had already made the acute observation that the torso is a part of the body which conceals organs; and Tàpies's tendency to show what is covered, or simply to cover, now becomes an extraction of matter in a return to the chiaroscuro of the Romantics (which presents the figure as something dreamed of) or to the brightness and transparency of varnish (which presents it as a bare sign and at the same time as something fleeting and remembered).

This is what we find, for instance, in *Cup* (Fig. 62), *Triangle of Varnish* (Fig. 68) and *Imprint of Sofa* (Fig. 76).

Signs

The presence of signs in Tàpies' work may come from memories or from synthesized ideas, and they also have a plastic logic of their own in the ensemble of the composition. Their meaning is manifold, as I have said before, depending on their relation to the other components of the picture. Thus, for instance, the figure-eights or bows in *Curved Forms* (Fig. 66) may easily become a chain. The painter is alluding to their spontaneous, automatic character, in which there is undoubtedly a constant accumulation of experiences — or echoes of emblems or symbols codified by tradition (which can, however, be subverted). Thus we see the appearance of

(m) Miró: *The Bird of the Beautiful Horizon*, 1969.

28

(n) Franz Kline: *Grave Accent,* 1955.

many typographical characters or other elements connected with writing, such as hyphens, brackets, commas, various letters and numbers — all of which, in combination with the painter's passion for paper, portfolios, slate, eyeglasses, etc., tell us of a personality greatly addicted to books and to what we might call the "aesthetic of stationery," of printing or of publishing (we should remember, besides, the bookselling and publishing tradition in his family).

We also find crosses, bows, angles, the four stripes of the Catalan flag, words (sometimes phrases) and an endless number of gestural scrawls and scribbles, from those of a most shapeless kind (mere tangles of lines) to suggestions of ears, mouths, noses, phalli, etc. Signs, strokes and stains have appeared, we must remember, in a great many works of art in this century: in Miró and Klee, in what has been called European gestural abstract art, in the American version of the same. In Tàpies they may be given a more openly emblematic significance, as in *The Catalan Spirit* (Fig. 37) or in *Madman* (Fig. 47), where he alludes to the theme of madness — which has impressed him since his childhood, in the dual aspect of attraction and repulsion — by means of the concept turned into words. The letters may be charged with metaphor or act as figures subjected to pressures; thus the *Large Y* (Fig. 67) has the solemnity of raised arms, while the O in *Red and Black* (Fig. 71) is imprisoned between two dark spaces.

Tàpies alternates the most energetic of gestures, similar in force and presence to that of Kline (n) or Motherwell in works like *Large Knot* (Fig. 75) or *Oblique Black Band* (Fig. 63), with a treatment of stains quite as subtle as that of some Japanese works, as in *Composition with India Ink* (Fig. 59). In this respect his knowledge and appreciation of eastern art (which was also highly esteemed by many Surrealist and non-figurative painters) cause him to use a technique that is similar to the original: a controlled haphazardness, in which a previous spiritual concentration prepares the way for a free gesture of the hand, as also the use or exploitation of accidents (dripping, stain) or the influence of music. In some recent works, however, we find once more a deliberate confusion of signs, a more clearly expressionistic mood, a profusion of stains and asymmetries, signs of skulls and spectral faces which recall, though with other means, the *Dau al Set* period, or which make us think of a sagacious integration of the latest expressionist styles. But we must not forget that these features already appeared, and very forcibly, in the lithographs for *Novel·la* (in collaboration with Joan Brossa) and that there are in fact certain works, especially those of the sixties, that seem to be antecedents for the recent neo-expressionist trends. A young artist like Julian Schnabel, for instance, reveals in some of his works a mixture of brutalism and refinement that is very close to the aesthetic of Tàpies.

BIOGRAPHICAL DATA

1923
Born in Barcelona, on 13th December, to the lawyer Josep Tàpies i Mestre and his wife, Maria Puig i Guerra.

1926-1931
Kindergarten, followed by primary schooling at the Loreto Convent, the German School and the school of the Piarist Fathers in Barcelona.

1934
Begins his secondary studies. First contact with contemporary art through the special Christmas issue of the magazine *D'Ací i D'Allà*, p. 12.

1936-1939
The Spanish Civil War. Continues his studies at the Liceo Práctico and the Instituto Menéndez y Pelayo. Works for some months at the Autonomous Government of Catalonia, where his father is employed as a legal adviser. Continues, self-taught, to practise drawing and painting.

1940
Returns to the Escuela Balmes of the Piarist Fathers, but his studies are frequently interrupted by his delicate state of health.

1942-1943
Develops a serious condition of the lungs and has to spend a long period of convalescence at the Sanatorium of Puig d'Olena. Copies works of Van Gogh and Picasso. Reads Thomas Mann, Wölfflin, Ibsen, Nietzsche, Spengler, etc. Becomes fond of Romantic music.

1944
Studies law at Barcelona University, but gives it up shortly before graduating. Studies drawing for two months at the Academia Valls in Barcelona.

1945
Paints with thick pigments which he obtains by mixing oil paint with whiting. Also does collages with pieces of rubbish, ropes, etc. Alternates abstraction and primitivism.

1947
Meets the poet Joan Brossa and a relationship of mutual influence at once begins between them. Also meets Joan Prats. First engravings.

1948
Exhibits two works at the Saló d'Octubre: *Painting* and *Collage of the Crosses* (1947). Together with Brossa, Ponç, Cuixart, Tharrats and Arnau Puig, founds the magazine *Dau al Set*. Takes an interest in Surrealism.

1949
Shows several works in an exhibition entitled *An Aspect of Catalan Painting*, organized by Cobalto 49 at the French Institute of Barcelona. On the invitation of Eugenio d'Ors, shows some works at the Salón de los Once in Madrid. Illustrates poems by Brossa and makes the acquaintance of J. V. Foix. His marked interest in Surrealism becomes noticeable in his painting. First contacts with eastern art and philosophy.

1950
First one-man show, organized by Josep Gudiol at the Galeries Laietanes, Barcelona. Brossa publishes his *Oracle sobre Antoni Tàpies* and Tharrats a monograph entitled *Tàpies o el dau modern de Versalles*. Goes to Paris with a scholarship awarded him by the French Government through the French Institute of Barcelona. Is selected for the Carnegie Prize and exhibits in Pittsburgh.

1951
Meets Picasso. Retrospective *Dau al Set* exhibition at the Sala Caralt, organized by Luis Sánchez Poveda. Dissolution of the *Dau al Set* group.

1952
Exhibits at the 26th Venice Biennale and is again invited to show at the Carnegie Institute. One-man show at the Galeries Laietanes. His painting shows a growing tendency to abstraction (geometrizing works and color studies).

1953
One-man shows in Chicago and Madrid. First visit to New York on the occasion of his exhibition at the Martha Jackson Gallery. Prize at the São Paulo Biennale. Resumes research on materials begun eight years earlier, working with clays, *grattage*, collage, incisions, etc.

1954
Exhibitions in several cities in the United States, organized by Martha Jackson. Also exhibits in Barcelona and at the 27th Venice Biennale. Publication of Alexandre Cirici's *Tàpies o la transverberació*. In Paris meets Michel Tapié. Marries Teresa Barba Fàbregas.

1955
Exhibitions in Stockholm and Barcelona. Participates in the exhibition *Phases de l'art contemporain* in Paris, organized by E. Jaquer. Signs a contract with the Galerie Stadler, Paris. Gives a lecture at the Summer University of Santander, which is later published under the title *La vocación y la forma*. Is awarded the Prize of the Republic of Colombia at the 3rd Hispano-American Biennale, held in Barcelona.

1956
Publication of Michel Tapié's *Antoni Tàpies et l'œuvre complète*. Shows at the Galerie Stadler in Paris. Goes more deeply into the study of eastern philosophy: Vedanta, Tantrism, Zen, Buddhism, etc. Birth of his son Antoni.

1957
Exhibitions in Paris and Dusseldorf. Is awarded the Lissone (Milan) first prize for young artists.

1958
One-man show at the Galleria dell'Ariete, Milan, presented by Jacques Dupin. Is given an individual room at the Venice Biennale. First prize of the Carnegie Institute, Pittsburgh, awarded by a committee composed of J.J. Sweeney, Marcel Duchamp (who Tàpies later meets through Joan Prats), Lionello Venturi, F.J. Kiesler, Mary Callery, Raoul Ubac and Vincent Price. Is awarded the UNESCO prize and the prize of the David Bright Foundation of Los Angeles. Exhibits in New York and at the Osaka Festival. Birth of his daughter Clara.

1959
Publication of the monograph *Antoni Tàpies*, by Michel Tapiè. One-man shows in New York, Washington, Paris, Bern and Munich.

1960

Publication of the monograph *Tàpies*, by J.E. Cirlot. The review *Papeles de Son Armadans*, edited by Camilo José Cela, devotes a special issue to his work. One-man shows in Barcelona and Bilbao. In the United States participates in the exhibitions *New Spanish Painting and Sculpture* (Museum of Modern Art, New York) and *Before Picasso, after Miró* (Guggenheim Museum, New York). Buys an old farmhouse in the Montseny district, where the family is to spend long periods of the year. Birth of his son Miquel.

1961

More one-man shows: New York, Washington, Essen, Munich, Paris, Buenos Aires, Stockholm and Venice.

1962

Werner Schmalenbach organizes his first retrospective exhibition, at the Kestner-Gesellschaft Museum in Hanover. Does stage sets for Brossa's play *Or i Sal*. Retrospective exhibitions at the Guggenheim Museum in New York and the Kunsthaus in Zurich. Paints a large mural for the library of the Handels-Hochschule, Sankt Gallen (Switzerland). One-man shows in Caracas, Rome and Stockholm. Publication of J.E. Cirlot's *Significación de la pintura de Tàpies*.

1963

Moves into his new house and studio (No. 57, Carrer de Saragossa, Barcelona), built for him by the architect Josep-Antoni Coderch. Publishes (in collaboration with Brossa) *El pa a la barca*. One-man shows in Pasadena, Paris, Turin, Sankt Gallen and New York. Prize of the Art Club of Providence, Rhode Island.

1964

One-man shows in Cologne, Paris, Rome and Barcelona. Participates in the exhibitions *Painting and Sculpture of a Decade* (Tate Gallery, London) and *España libre* (Rimini, Florence, Reggio Emilia, Venice and Ferrara). Is given an individual room at Documenta III in Kassel. Blai Bonet publishes *Tàpies*. J. Teixidor publishes *Antoni Tàpies: Fustes, cartons, papers, collages*.

1965

One-man shows in Cologne and London. Publication of his *Novel·la*, done in collaboration with Joan Brossa.

1966

Participates in the meeting of intellectuals held at the Capuchin Monastery in Sarrià, for which he is arrested and fined. Begins to write his memoirs and writes increasingly in the press. One-man shows in Madrid, Paris, Stockholm, Cannes and Toulouse. At the Menton Biennale is awarded the *Grand Prix du Président de la République*.

1967

Signs a contract with the Galerie Maeght, Paris, where he exhibits in November. Grand Prix for Engraving at the Ljubljana (Yugoslavia) Biennale. Collaborates with Jacques Dupin on the book *La Nuit grandissante*. Publication of *Antoni Tàpies o l'escarnidor de diademes*, a book edited by Joan Prats with photographs by Joaquim Gomis and text by Francesc Vicens and Joan Brossa. Exhibition at the Kunstmuseum of Sankt Gallen. Publication in Italy of the monograph *Antoni Tàpies*, with text by Giuseppe Gatt, Argan, Barilli, Calvesi, Menna, Ponente and Tomassoni. Ralph Wuhlin makes the film *Antoni Tàpies* for Swedish television.

1968

Anthological exhibition in Vienna (Museum des 20. Jahrhunderts), Hamburg (Kunstverein) and Cologne (Kunstverein). One-man shows in Paris and New York. Does some screens with pieces of sheets for the windows of the Capuchin Monastery of Sion, Switzerland.

1969

Publishes *Frègoli*, done in collaboration with Brossa. Clovis Prevost makes the film *Antoni Tàpies*, produced by the Maeght Foundation. J.M. Acarín and A. Dañhel make the film *Malír Tàpies* for Czech television. One-man shows in Paris and Barcelona.

1970

Visits Montserrat to express his solidarity with those who have staged a sit-in there to protest against the Burgos trials. Does some new assemblages and his first sculptures. Does a mural in Sankt Gallen for the town's new theater. Alexandre Cirici publishes *Tàpies, testimoni del silenci*. Publication of *La pràctica de l'art*, a selection of the painter's writings and declarations.

1971

One-man shows in Barcelona, New York and Rome. Does 14 etchings to illustrate André du Bouchet's poem, *Air*.

1972

One-man shows in Paris and in Siegen (West Germany), where he is awarded the Rubens Prize.

1973

Retrospective exhibitions in Paris (Musée National d'Art Moderne) and Charleroi (Palais des Beaux-Arts). Mariuccia Galfetti publishes *Tàpies, obra gráfica 1947-1972*. Illustrations for *La clau del foc*, by Pere Gimferrer. Publication of *Suite Catalana* and, with Brossa, of *Poems from the Catalan*.

1974

Publication of *L'art contra l'estètica*, a second selection of the artist's writings and declarations. Is awarded the Prize of the British Arts Council at the International Engraving Exhibition in England. Retrospective exhibitions in Copenhagen (Louisiana Museum) and Berlin (Neue Nationalgalerie). Presentation in Paris of the series of monotypes entitled *Assassins*. Publication of *Cartes per a la Teresa*, a book consisting of 52 lithographs and collages. Is awarded the Stephan-Lochner-Medaille by the city of Cologne. Werner Schmalenbach publishes *Antoni Tàpies Zeichen und Strukturen*. Pere Gimferrer publishes *Antoni Tàpies i l'esperit català*.

1975

Illustrations for *Llambrec material*, by the Japanese poet Takuguchi: X», by Jean Daive; *Ça suit son cours*, by Edmond Jabés; and *Oda a Xirinachs*, by Joan Brossa.

1976

Retrospective exhibitions in Saint-Paul-de-Vence (Fondation Maeght), Tokyo (Seibu Museum) and Barcelona (Fundació Joan Miró). At the Venice Biennale participates in the special show entitled *Spagna: Avanguardia artistica e realità sociale 1936-1976*. Publication of the monograph *Tàpies*, by Georges Raillard.

1977

Travelling retrospective exhibition in the United States and Canada (Albright-Knox Art Gallery, Buffalo, New York; Museum of Contemporary Art, Chicago, Illinois; Marion Koogler McNay Art Institute, San Antonio, Texas; Des Moines Art Center, Des Moines, Iowa; Musée d'Art Contemporain, Montreal, Quebec). Publication of the monograph *Tàpies*, by Roland Penrose. Retrospective exhibition of the artist's work on paper in Bremen (Kunsthalle) and Baden-Baden (Staatliche Kunsthalle).

1978

Retrospective exhibition of the artist's work on paper in Winterthur, Switzerland (Kunstmuseum) and Les Sables d'Olonne, France (Abbaye Sainte-Croix). Publishes *Memòria personal*, an autobiography. Illustrates Rafael Alberti's *Retornos de lo vivo lejano*. Illustrates Alexander Mitscherlich's *Sinnieren über Schmutz*. One-man shows in Madrid, Sankt Gallen, Paris and Barcelona.

1979

City of Barcelona Award. Pablo Antonio Olavide Prize for testimonial literature, awarded by the Club Master for *Memòria personal*. Is elected an honorary member of the Berlin Academy of Fine Arts. With Joan Brossa, publishes the book *U no és ningú*. Does eight etchings to illustrate Octavio Paz's book *Petrificada*,

Petrificante. Retrospective exhibition in Karlsruhe (Badischer Kunsthalle), on the occasion of which A. Franzke and M. Schwarz publish *Antoni Tàpies. Werk und Zeit.*

1980
Retrospective exhibitions in Kiel (Kunsthalle), Linz (Neue Galerie), Madrid (Museo de Arte Contemporáneo) and Amsterdam (Stedelijk Museum). Does six etchings to illustrate Jorge Guillén's *Repertorio de junio.* One-man shows in Rome, Málaga and Zürich.

1981
In Madrid is awarded the gold medal of the Directorate General of Fine Arts and Archives. Is given an honorary doctorate by the Royal College of Art, London. Publication of *Conversaciones con Tàpies,* by Miguel Fernández-Braso. Retrospective exhibition at the Fondation du Château de Jau. One-man shows in Osaka, New York, San Francisco, Mexico, Barcelona and Madrid. In Cologne participates in the exhibition *Zur spanischen Situation-1939 bis 1980.* The City Hall of Barcelona commissions him to do a monument to Picasso.

1982
Retrospective exhibition at the Scuola di San Giovanni Evangelista, on the occasion of the Venice Biennale (catalogue with texts by Carmine Benincasa, Maurizio Calvesi and Vittorio Sgarbi). Does the décor for Jacques Dupin's play *L'Éboulement.* Is awarded (with Marc Chagall) the prize of the Wolf Foundation of Jerusalem. Illustrates Pere Gimferrer's *Aparicions.* Publication of *Tàpies, répliquer,* by Jean Daive. Josep Vallès publishes *Tàpies emprenta (Art, Vida).* One-man shows in Rome, Barcelona, Saragossa, New York, Salzburg and Munich.

1983
Unveiling of the monument to Picasso in Barcelona, with various lectures and an exhibition on the subject in the assembly hall of the University. Does a mosaic for the Plaça de Catalunya in Sant Boi. Exhibits at the Abbaye de Sénanque, Gordes (France). The works presented are basically characterized by the use of inks and varnishes on flat surfaces, materials which the painter has been making considerable use of in recent years. Is awarded the gold medal of the *Generalitat* (Autonomous Government) of Catalonia. Is awarded the Rembrandt Prize by the M. Toepfer Foundation of Berlin at its seat in Basel. Is named "Officier de l'Ordre des Arts et des Lettres" by the French Government for his contribution to the world of culture.

1984
Inaugurates his exhibitions of ceramic sculptures done between 1981 and 1983 at the Galerie Maeght Lelong, Zürich. New one-man show at the Galerie Maeght Lelong, Paris. Publication of the book *Els cartells de Tàpies,* with a text by Rosa Maria Malet and cataloguing by Miquel Tàpies. Victòria Combalia publishes her monograph *Tàpies.* Awarded the Peace Prize by the Spanish branch of the Association for United Nations. Publishes in "La Vanguardia" a long series of articles in which he defends artistic and cultural modernity. One-man shows in Lyon, Paris, Madrid, Stockholm, Seoul, Saporo, Tokyo, Nagoya, Osaka, Hiroshima and Fukuoka. The Antoni Tàpies Foundation is created.

1985
Goes to Milan where he attends the opening of the *Tàpies Milano* exhibition, organized by the City Council. Publication of the book *Llull* (a project begun in 1973) with engravings by Tàpies,

a selection of texts by Pere Gimferrer and an epilogue by Miquel Batllori. Publishes *Per un art modern i progresista.* In the autumn he goes to Brussels, where he inaugurates his one-man show included as part of *Europalia 85.* Receives the Swiss Internationale Triennale für farbige Originalgrafik de Grenchen Award. Goes to Paris, where he receives the Prix National de Peinture from the French Government. Is made member of the Stockholm Royal Academy of Fine Arts. One-man shows in Barcelona, Madrid, Düsseldorf, Helsinki, Knokke-le-Zoute and Paris.

1986
Goes to Vienna, where he opens a new anthological exhibition at the Wienes Künstlerhaus. Rudi Fuchs, who chose the works exhibited, writes the catalog preface. Later the exhibition travels to the Van Abbemuseum, Eindhoven. Participates in the exhibition-homage *A Joan Miró* at the Joan Miró Foundation, Barcelona. Participates in the inaugural exhibition of the Centro de Arte Reina Sofía, Madrid. Retrospective exhibition at the Galería Theo, Madrid. Exhibits new sculptures and ceramic mural reliefs at the Montmajour Abbey, Arles. One-man shows in Madrid and Barcelona.

1987
The Antoni Tàpies Foundation signs agreements with the *Generalitat* of Catalonia and the Barcelona City Hall. Barbara Catoir publishes *Gespräche mit Antoni Tàpies.* Takes part in the *Le siècle de Picasso* exhibition at the Musée d'Art Moderne de la Ville de Paris, and in the *Fifty Years of Collecting: An Anniversary Selection. Painting since World War II* exhibition at the Solomon R. Guggenheim Museum, New York. One-man shows in New York, Madrid, Zürich, Valencia, Cologne and Hannover.

1988
Invested "Doctor Honoris Causa" by the University of Barcelona. The City Hall of Barcelona organizes the exhibition *Tàpies: els anys 80* at the Saló del Tinell, which subsequently travels to Palma de Mallorca under the auspices of the University of the Balearic Islands. Anthological exhibition at the Musée Cantini, Marseilles. Anna Agustí publishes *Tàpies. Obra Completa, 1943-1960,* the first volume of the general catalogue of Tàpies' works. He participates in the *Aspects of Collage, Aseemblage and the Found Object in Twentieth-Century Art* exhibition at the Solomon R. Guggenheim Museum, New York. Exhibits together with Kounellis and Richard Serra at the Jean Bernier Gallery, Athens. Takes part in the *Le Défi Catalan* show at the Château de Biron, Dordogne. Retrospective exhibition of his graphic works in different universities in the USA. One-man shows in Paris, Basel, London, Barcelona, Sankt Gallen and Rome.

1989
Made honorary member of the Künstlerhaus, Vienna. Travels to New York where he attends the inauguration of his new one-man exhibition at the Galerie Lelong. In Dusseldorf participates in the exhibition *Die Achtziger Jahre* (Nordrheim-Westfalen, Dusseldorf). Publication of *La réalité comme art* (Daniel Lelong Éditeur).

1990
One-man shows of new work on paper at the Galerie Lelong, New York, and new paintings at the Galerie Lelong, Paris. Exhibition in Chicago at the Richard Gray Gallery. Group show with Kounellis, Serra, Ruckriem at the Donal Young Gallery, Chicago.

BRIEF BIBLIOGRAPHY

AGUSTÍ, A.: *Tàpies. Obra Completa. Volum 1er. 1943-1960.* Fundació Antoni Tàpies and Edicions Polígrafa, Barcelona, 1988.

AINAUD I ESCUDERO, J.-F.: *Introducció a l'estètica d'Antoni Tàpies.* Edicions 62, Barcelona, 1986.

ALBEE, E.: Catalogue, Martha Jackson Gallery, New York, 1962.

ALLOWAY, L.: *Antoni Tàpies.* Catalogue, The Solomon R. Guggenheim Museum, New York, 1962.

ALTHAUS, P. F.: *Neue Aspekte der Iconographie im Werk von Antoni Tàpies.* Catalogue, Kunsthalle, Bremen, 1977.

ARGAN, G. C.: *La superstizione di Tàpies.* Catalogue, Instituto Torcuato di Tella, Buenos Aires, 1961.

BARRIO-GARAY, J. L.: *Intention, object and signification in the work of Tàpies.* Catalogue, The Albright-Knox Art Gallery, Buffalo, New York, 1977.

BROSSA, J.: *Oracle sobre Antoni Tàpies.* "Dau al Set," Barcelona, 1950.

CATOIR, B.: *Zu den Zeichnungen von Antoni Tàpies.* Catalogue, Kunsthalle, Bremen, 1977.
Gespräche mit Antoni Tàpies. Prestel-Verlag, Munich, 1987.

CIRICI, A.: *Tàpies, testimoni del silenci.* Edicions Polígrafa, Barcelona, 1970.

CIRLOT, J. E.: *Tàpies.* Omega, Barcelona, 1960.
Significación de la pintura de Tàpies. Seix Barral, Barcelona, 1962.

COMBALIA, V., and LOMBA, C.: *Tàpies.* Sarpe, Madrid, 1988.

DUPIN, J.: *Antoni Tàpies, papiers et cartons.* Catalogue, Galerie Berggruen, Paris, 1962.
"Tàpies aujourd'hui. Assemblages et objets." In *Derrière le miroir*, Galerie Maeght, Paris, 1967.

GALFETTI, M.: *Tàpies. Obra gráfica 1947-1972* (with an introduction by C. Vogel). Gustavo Gili, Barcelona, 1973.
Tàpies. Obra gráfica 1973-1978. Gustavo Gili, Barcelona, 1980.

GASCH, S.: *Tàpies.* Dirección General de Bellas Artes, Madrid, 1971.

GATT, G.; ARGAN, G. C.; CALVESI, M. et al.: *Antoni Tàpies.* Capelli, Bologna, 1967.

GIMFERRER, P.: *Tàpies i l'esperit català.* Edicions Polígrafa, 1976.

JARDÍ, E.: *Antoni Tàpies.* Ariel, Barcelona, 1950.

LINHARTOVÁ, V.: *Antoni Tàpies.* Verlag Gerd Hatje, Stuttgart, 1972.

LLORENS, T.: *Notes sobre la pintura de Tàpies.* Catalogue, Fundació Joan Miró, Barcelona, 1976.

MALET, R. M, and TÀPIES, M.: *Tàpies. Affiches.* Cercle d'Art, Paris, 1988.

PENROSE, R.: *Tàpies.* Edicions Polígrafa, Barcelona, 1977.

PERMANYER, L.: *Tàpies según la crítica.* Catalogue, Museo Español de Arte Contemporáneo, Madrid, 1980.

PLATSCHEK, H.: Catalogue, Im Erker Galerie, Sankt Gallen, 1973.

RAILLARD, G.: *Tàpies.* Maeght Éditeur, Paris, 1976.

SCHMALENBACH, W.: *Antoni Tàpies. Zeichen und Struckturen.* Propyläen Verlag, Berlin, 1974.

SWEENEY, J. J.: *Tàpies. A Catalogue of Paintings in America, 1950-1960.* Gres Gallery, Washington, 1961.

TAPIE, M.: *Antoni Tàpies.* R. M. Barcelona, 1959.
Antoni Tàpies. Fratelli Fabbri, Milan, 1969.

TEIXIDOR, J.: *Antoni Tàpies. Fustes, papers, cartons i collages.* Sala Gaspar, Barcelona, 1964.

THARRATS, J. J.: *Antoni Tàpies o el Dau Modern de Versalles.* "Dau al Set," Barcelona, 1950.

VARIOUS AUTHORS: "Papeles de Son Armadans." No. LVII, Madrid-Palma, 1960.

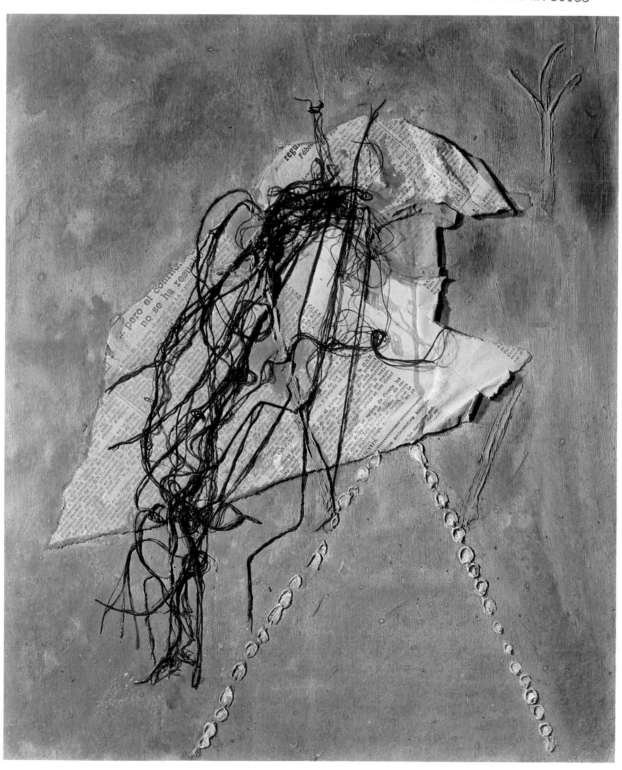

1. FIGURE OF NEWSPRINT AND THREADS. 1946-1947.

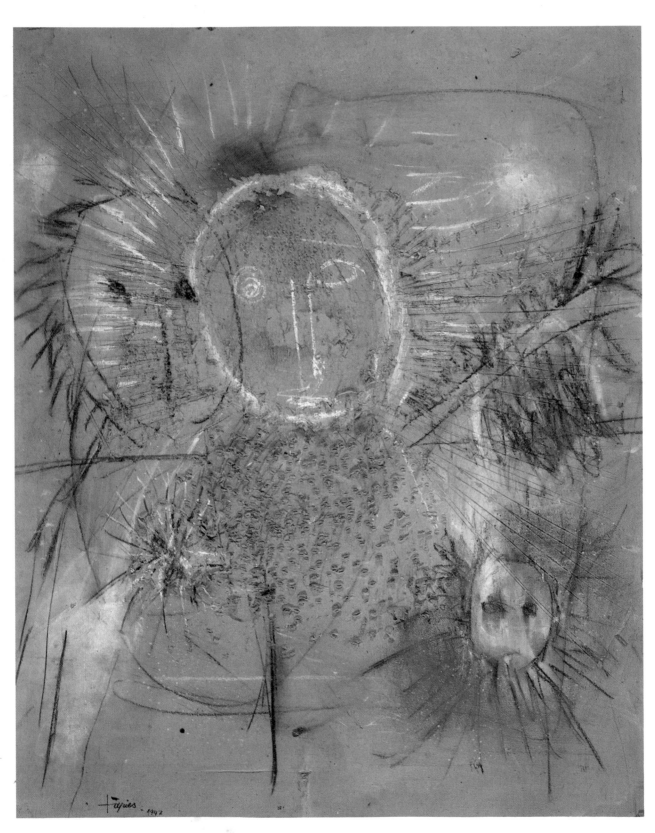

2. "GRATTAGE" ON CARDBOARD. 1947.

3. COLLAGE OF THE CROSSES. 1947.

4. PORTRAIT OF JOAN BROSSA. 1950-1970.

5.   NOURISHMENT. 1950.

6.   THE LEGERDEMAIN OF WOTAN. 1950.

7.   BANK NOTE COLLAGE. 1951.

8. THE AMPHORA. 1952.

9. WHITE WITH RED STAINS. 1954.

10.   PAINT WITH RED CROSS. 1954.

11. LARGE OVAL, 1956.

12.   LARGE GRAY PAINTING. 1955.

13. PAINTING No. XXVIII. 1955.

14. HIEROGLYPHICS. 1958-1960.

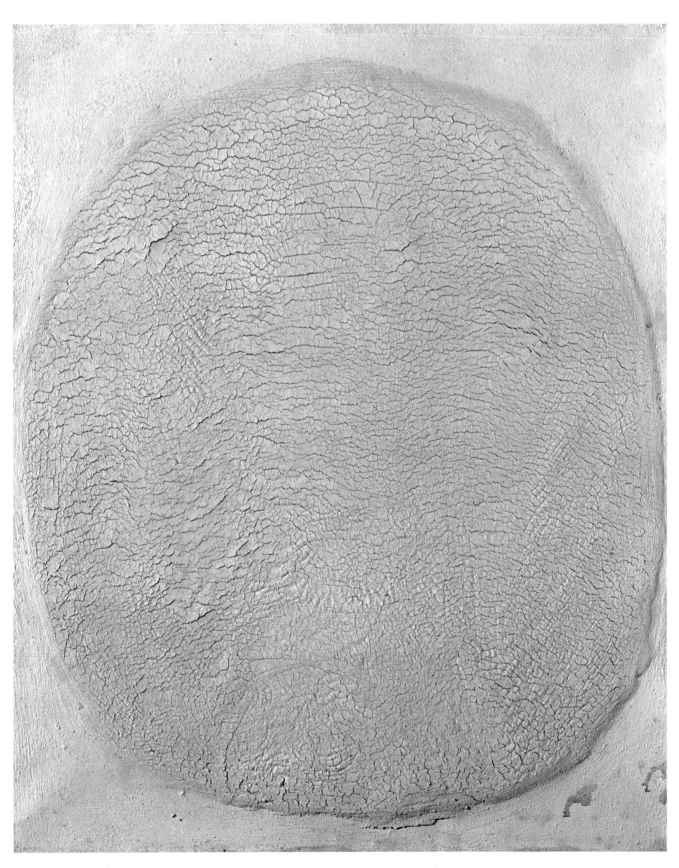

15.   WHITE OVAL. 1957.

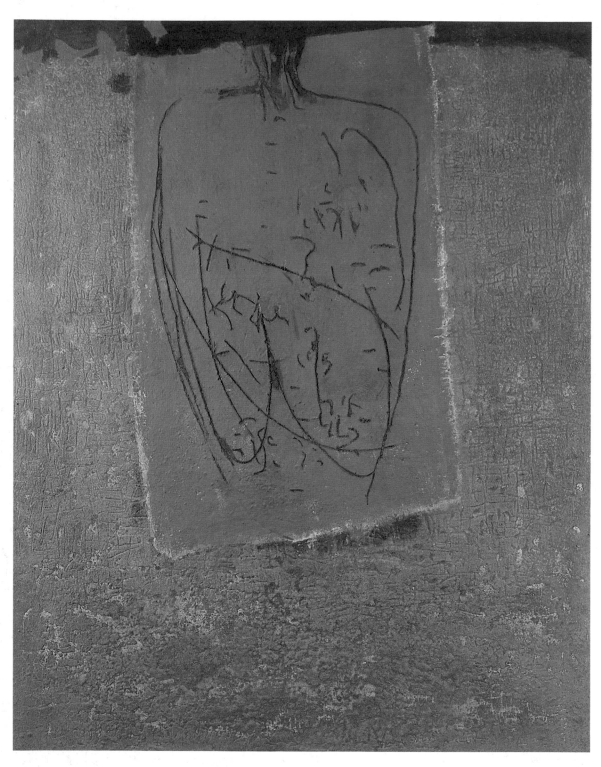

16.   LANDSCAPE-FIGURE IN RED. 1956.

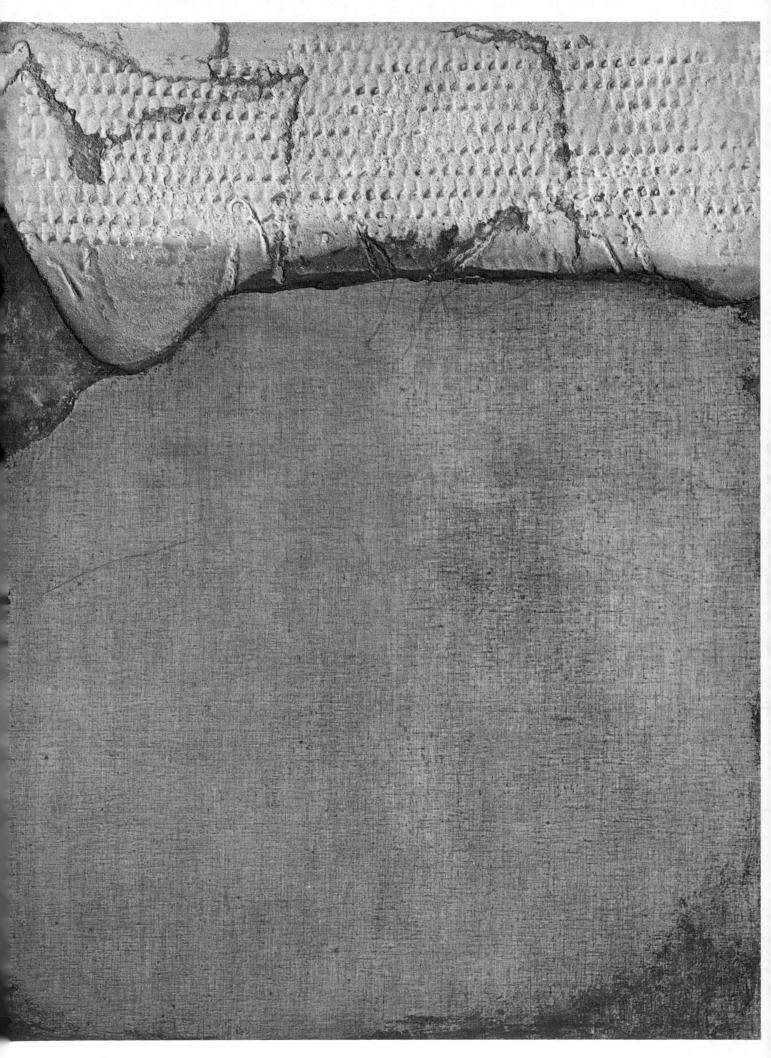

17.   GRAY FRAGMENT ON CANVAS. 1958.

18.   WHITE RELIEF. 1959.

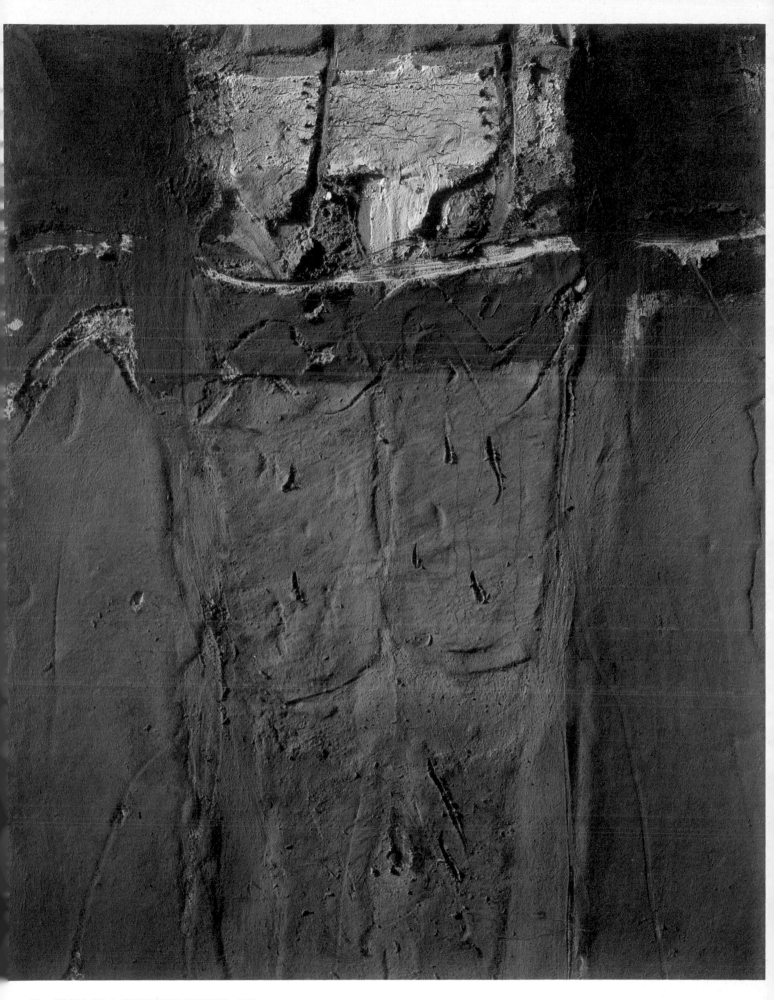

19.   FORM OF A CRUCIFIED FIGURE. 1959.

20. ALL WHITE WITH ARCS. 1960.

21. WHITE AND OCHER ON BROWN. 1961.

22.   BROWN BED. 1960.

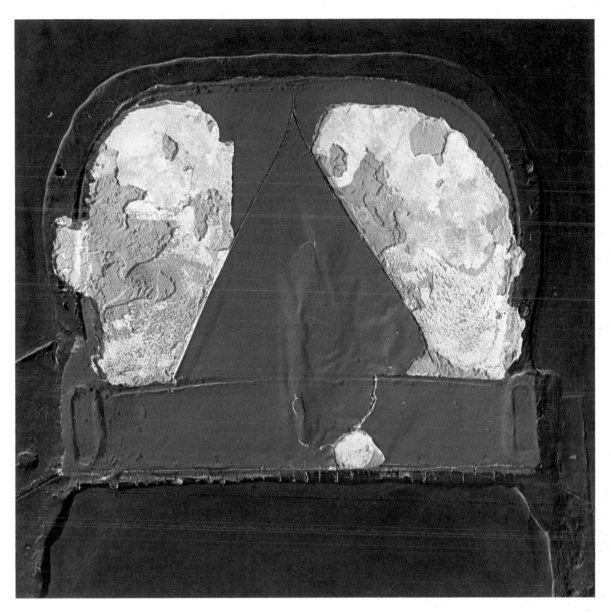

23.   RED AND BLACK WITH PATCHES TORN OFF. 1963-1965.

24.   LARGE MATERIAL WITH SIDE PAPERS. 1063.

25. OCHER AND PINK RELIEF. 1965.

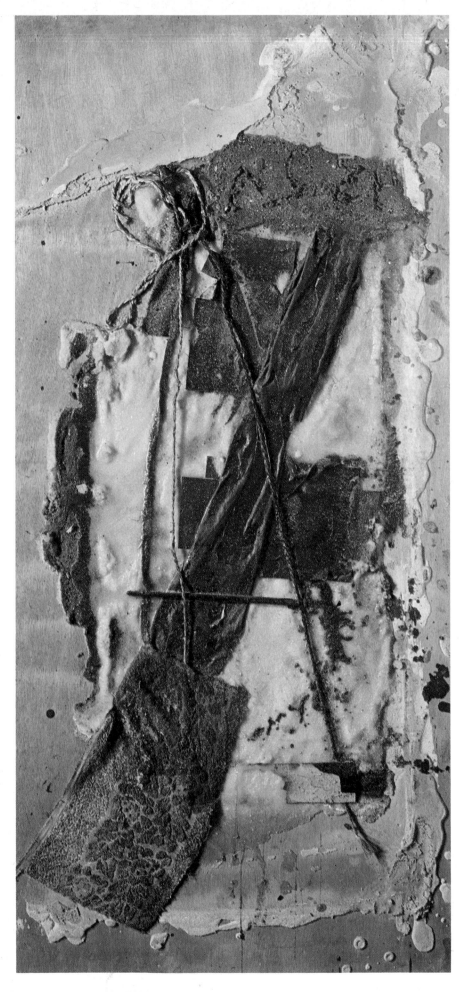

26. RAGS AND STRINGS ON PANEL. 1967.

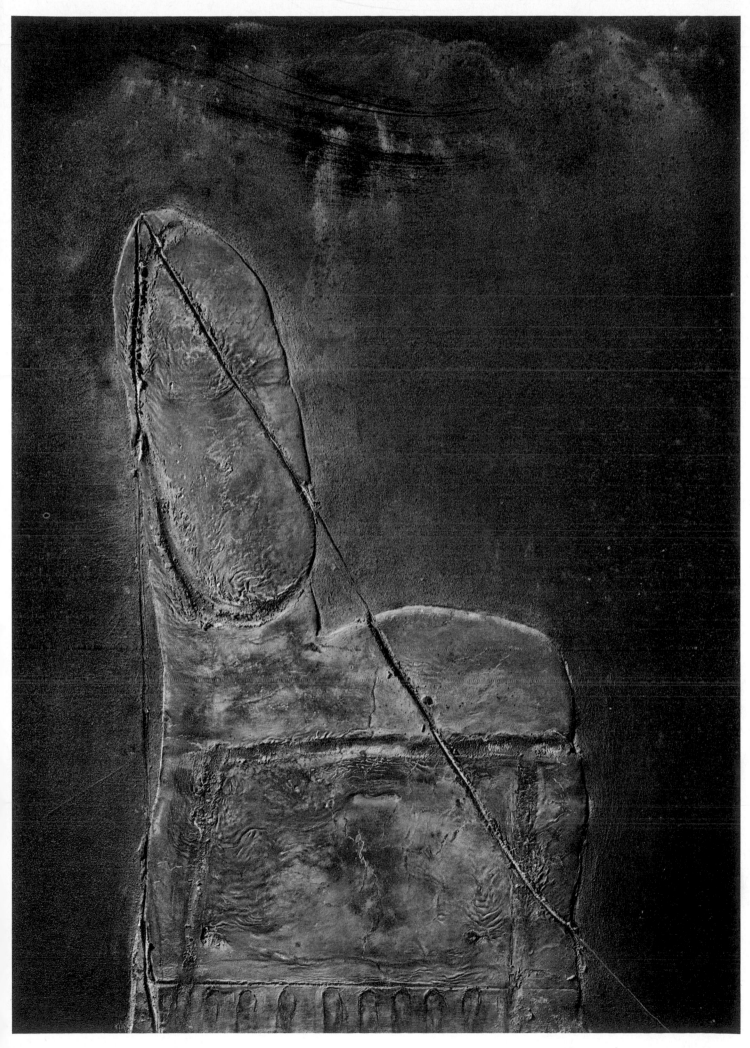

27. IN THE SHAPE OF A CHAIR. 1966.

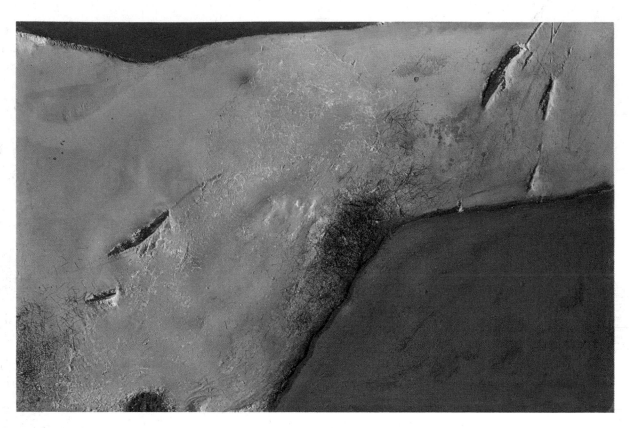

28.   MATERIAL IN THE SHAPE OF AN ARMPIT. 1968.

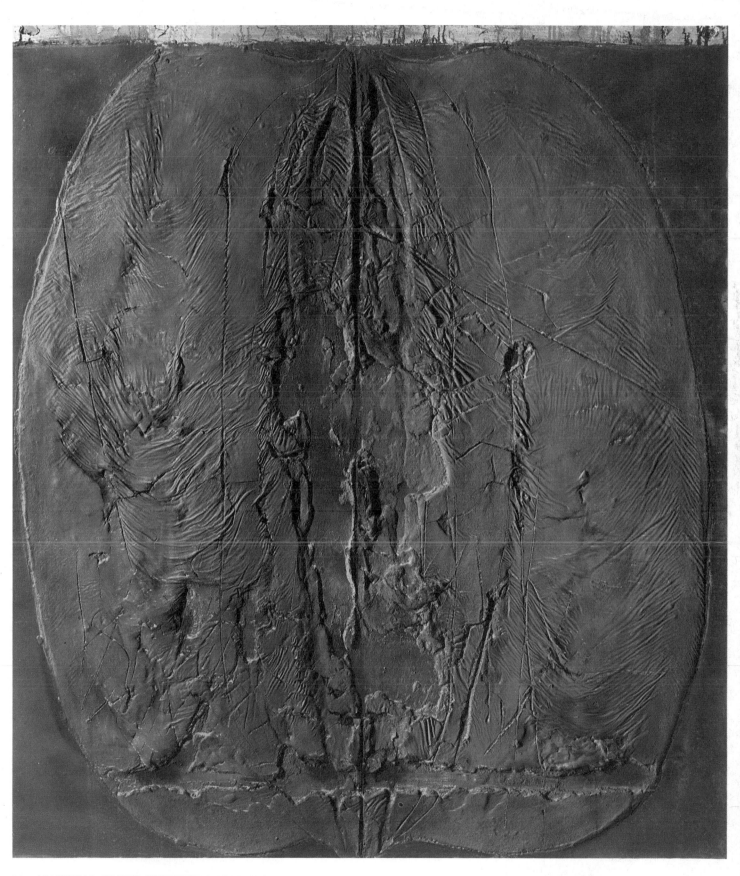

29. MATERIAL IN THE SHAPE OF A NUT. 1967.

30. LARGE DOOR. 1969.

31. STRAW AND WOOD. 1969.

32. STRETCHER COVERED WITH PLASTIC. 1968.

33. BODY OF MATERIAL AND ORANGE-COLORED STAINS. 1968.

34. BLACK AND EARTH. 1970.

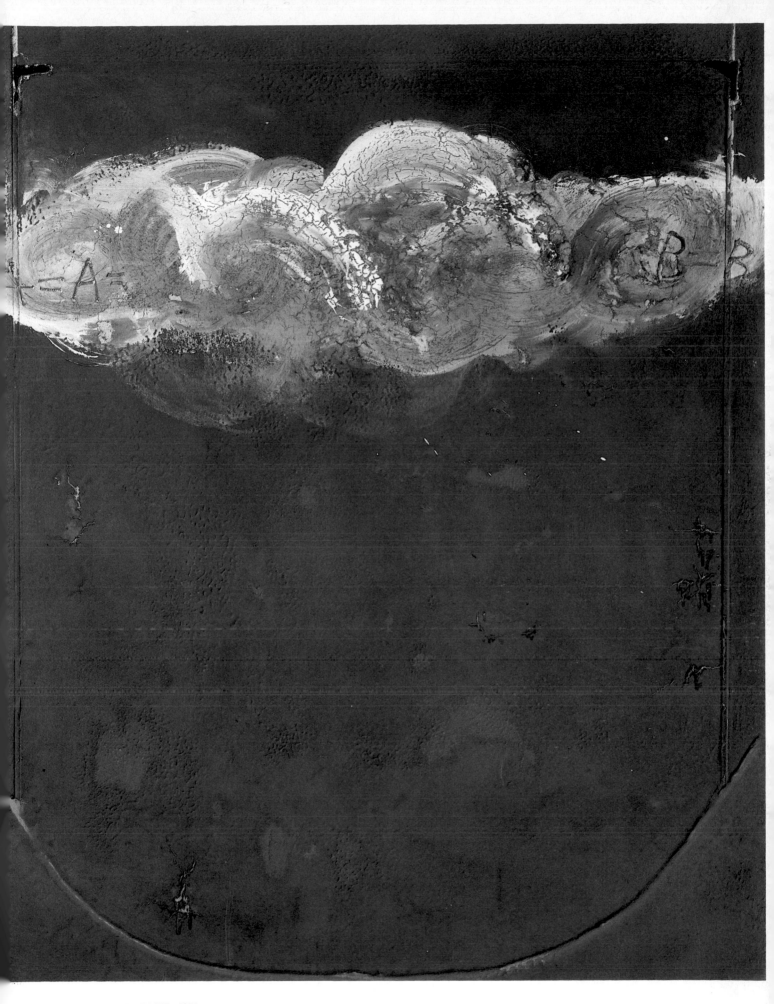

35. EMBLEMATIC BLUE. 1971.

36.   BLUE AND SACK. 1970.

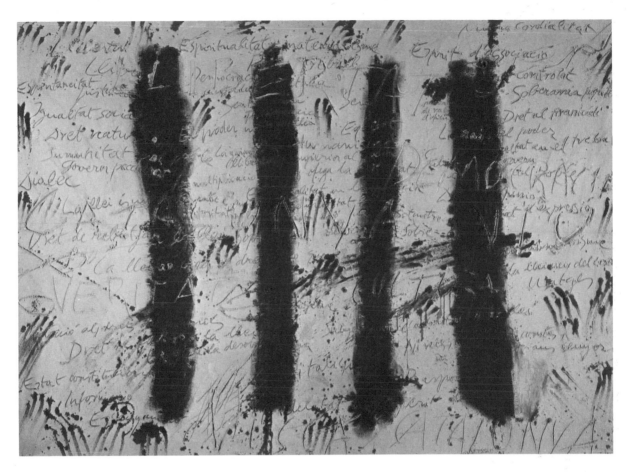

37.   THE CATALAN SPIRIT. 1971.

38.   LARGE PARCEL OF STRAW. 1969.

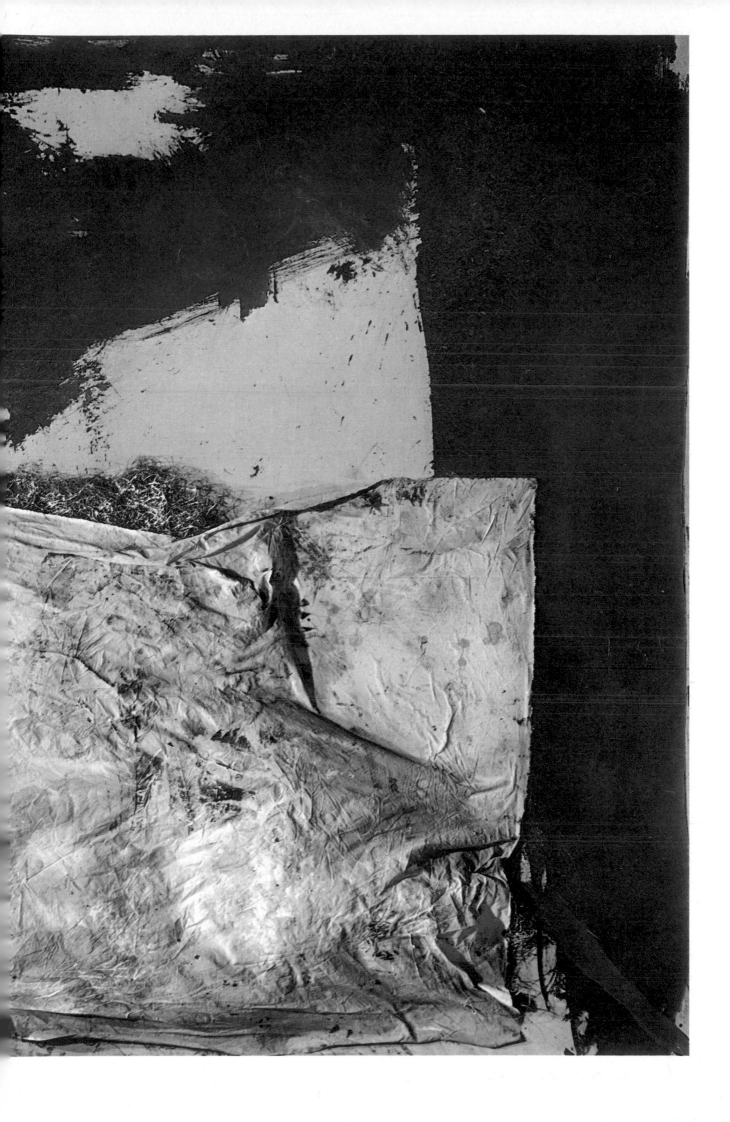

39.   MIRROR AND COLLAGE. 1971.

40. TWO BLACK CROSSES. 1973.

41. OCHER, BROWN AND WHITE WITH FOURS. 1972.

42. STAGE DÉCOR. 1974.

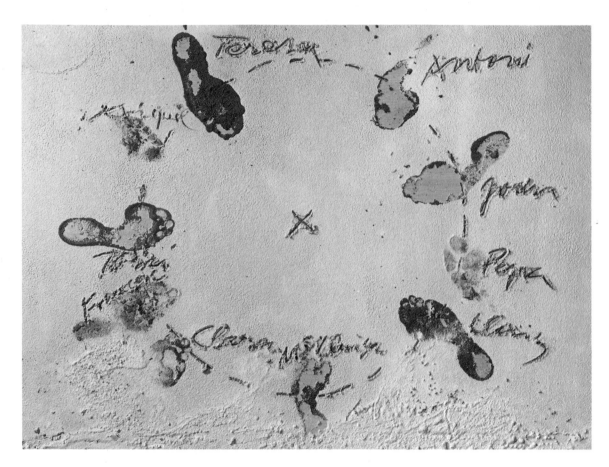

43. SARDANA-CIRCLE OF FEET. 1972.

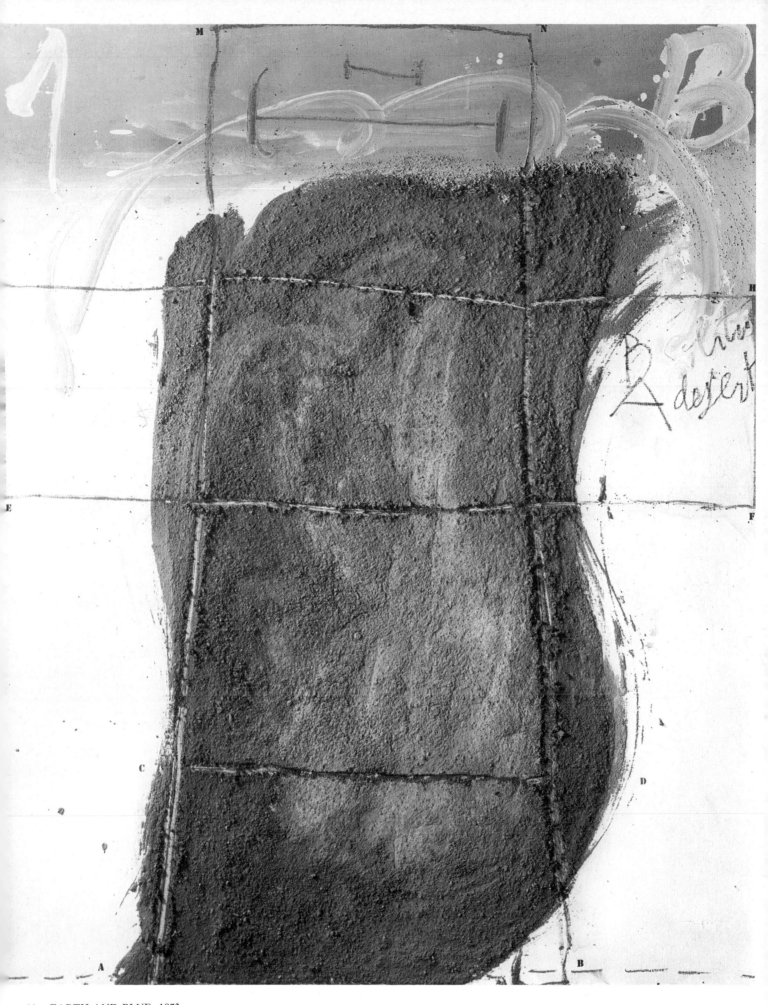

44.   EARTH AND BLUE. 1973.

45. PIECE OF CLOTH. 1973.

46.   WARDROBE DOOR. 1973.

47. MADMAN. 1973.

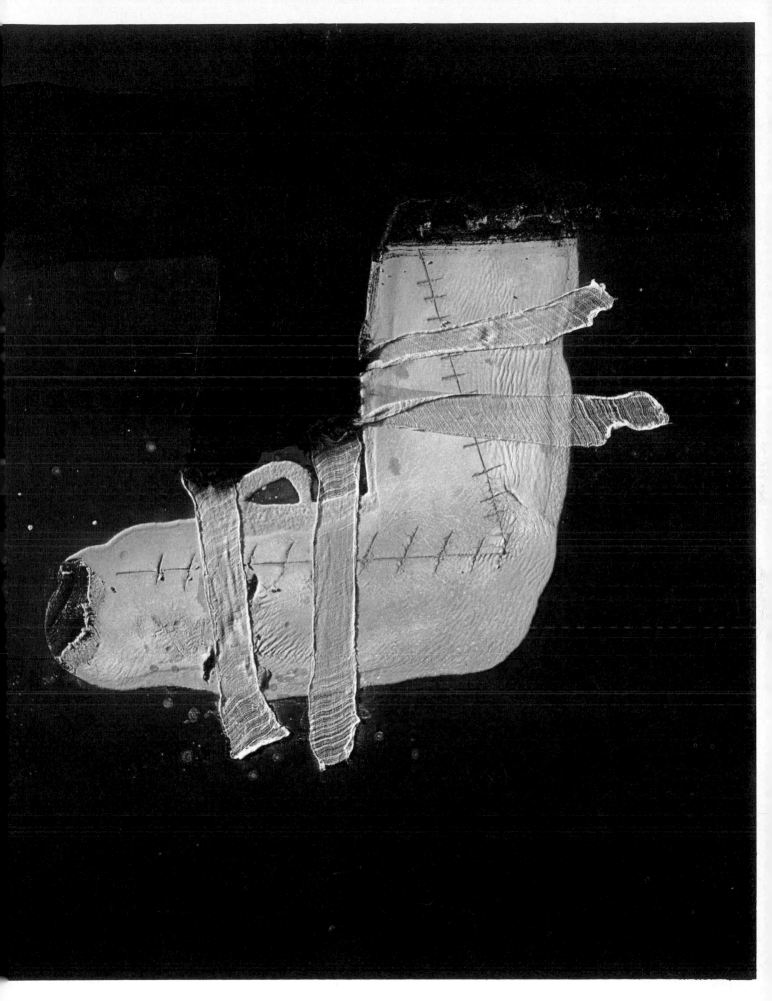

48.   ELBOW-MATERIAL. 1973.

49.   THE LADDER. 1974.

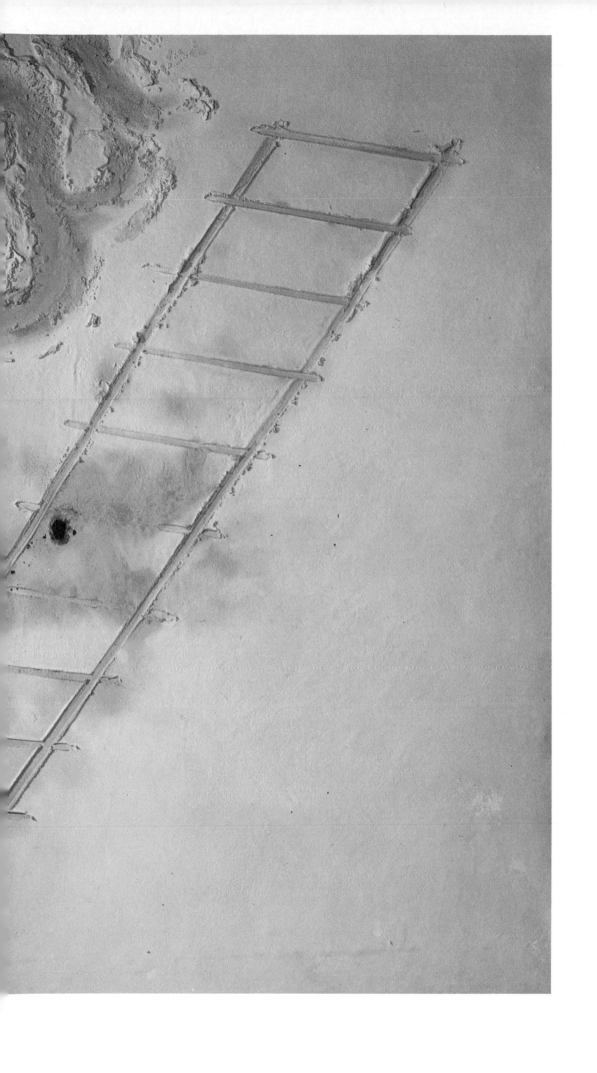

50. SÍ. 1974.

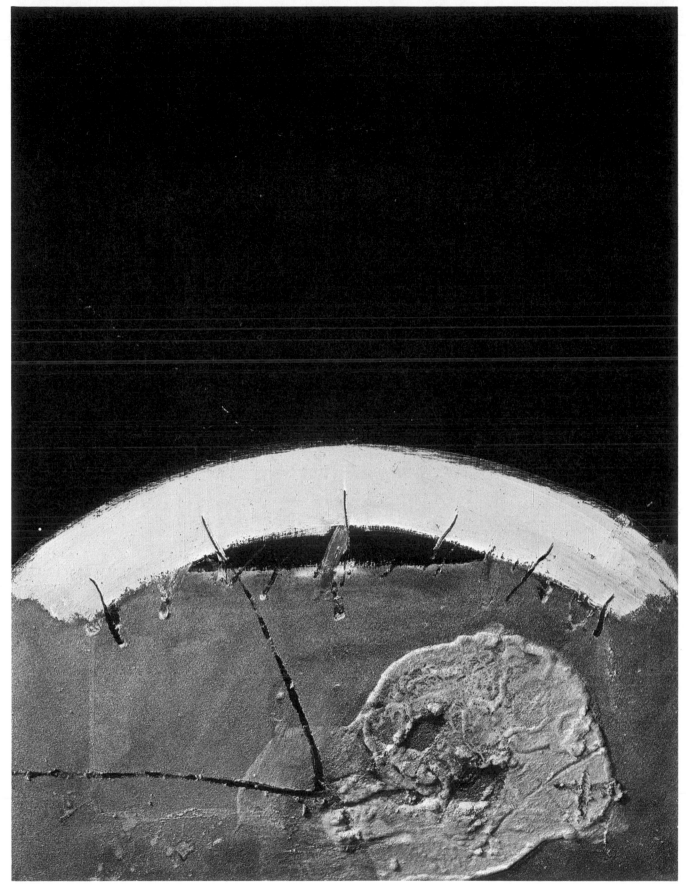

51. BLUE ARC. 1974.

52.   CORK-OAK GROVE. 1975.

53.   SQUARE ON SQUARE. 1976.

54. BLANKET WITH WHITE BAND. 1976.

55. GRAY AND ORANGE. 1977.

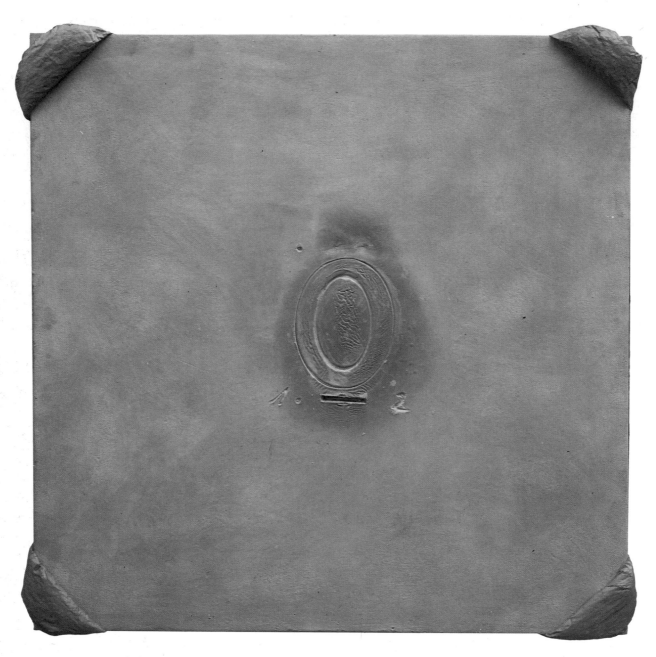

56. OVAL 1-2. 1978.

57. "ET AMICORUM." 1978.

58.   EFFECT OF STICK IN RELIEF. 1979.

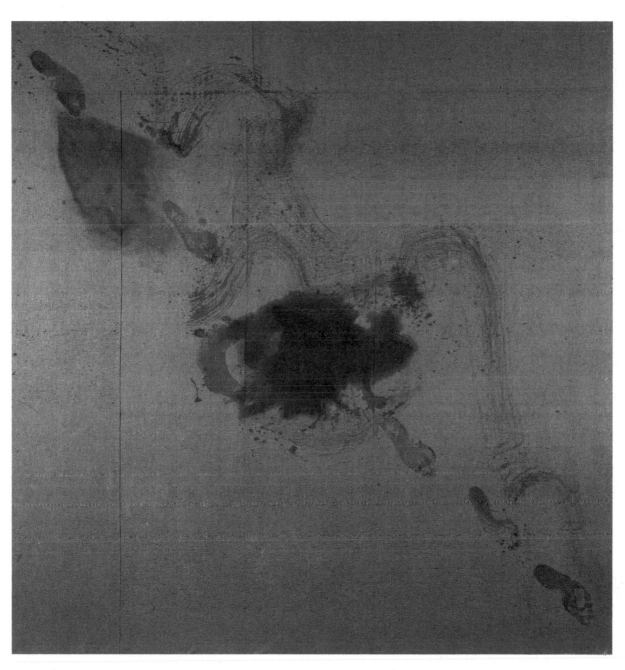

59.   COMPOSITION WITH INDIA INK. 1979.

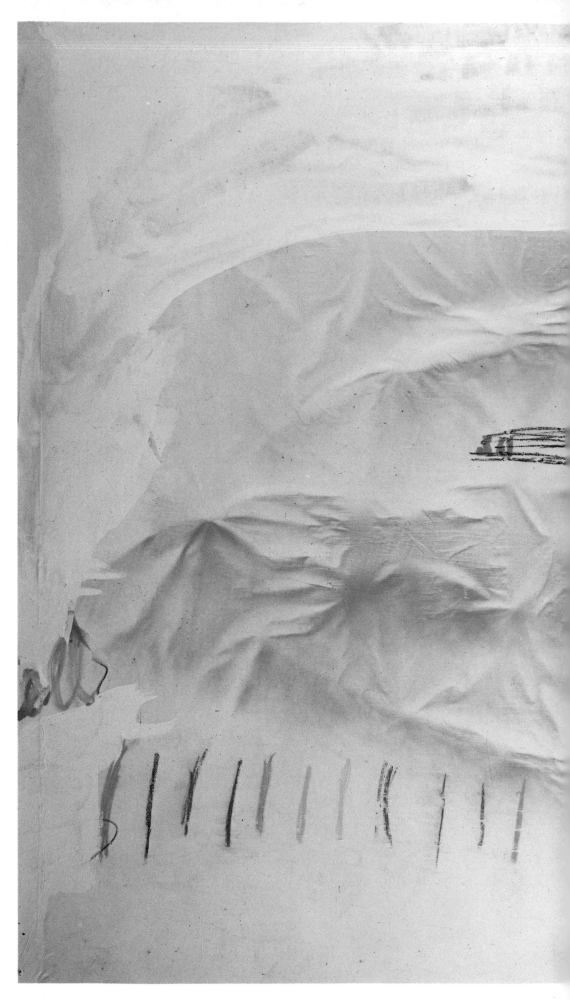

60.   EFFECT OF BODY IN RELIEF. 1979.

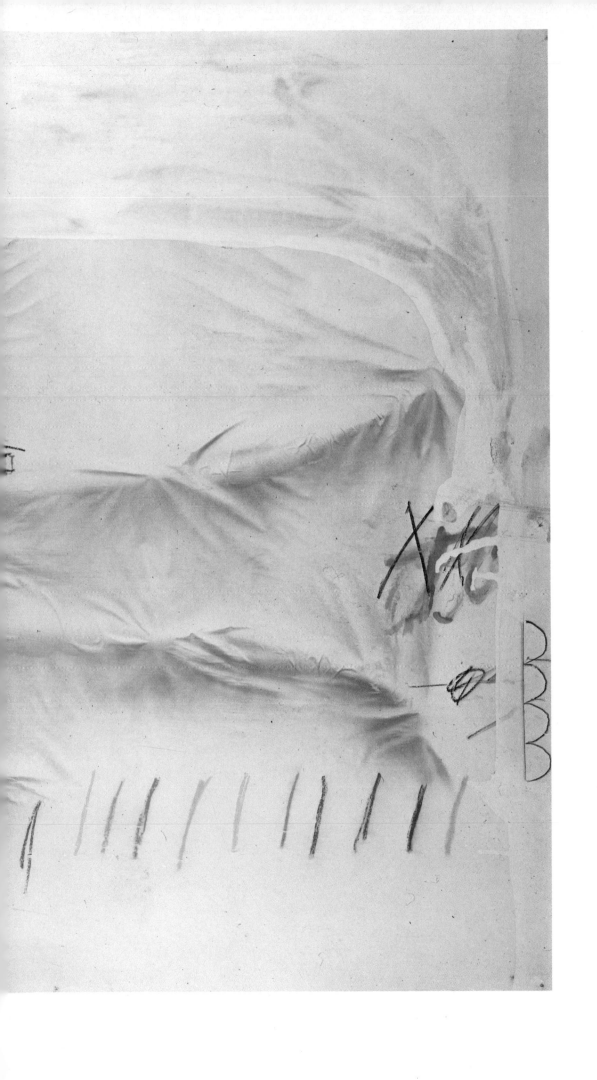

61. SUBJECT-OBJECT. 1979.

62. CUP. 1979.

63. OBLIQUE BLACK BAND. 1979.

4. BLUE AND TWO CROSSES. 1980.

65. BLACK ON GRAY MATERIAL. 1980.

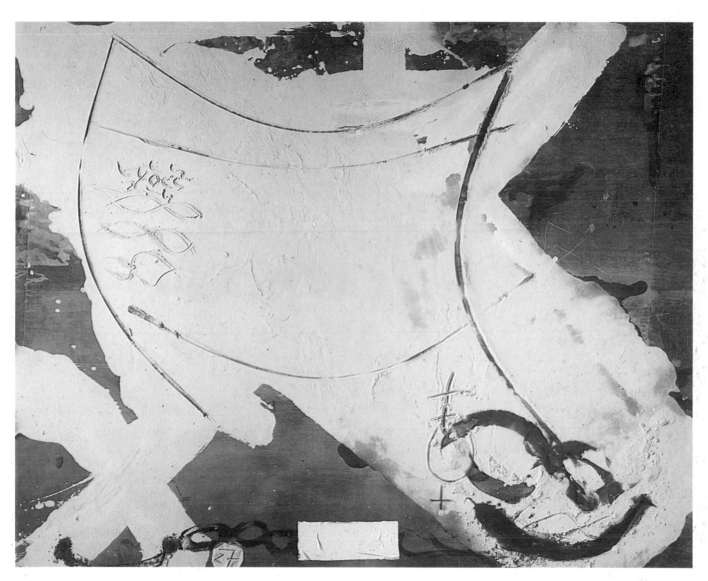

66. CURVED FORMS. 1980.

67. LARGE Y. 1980.

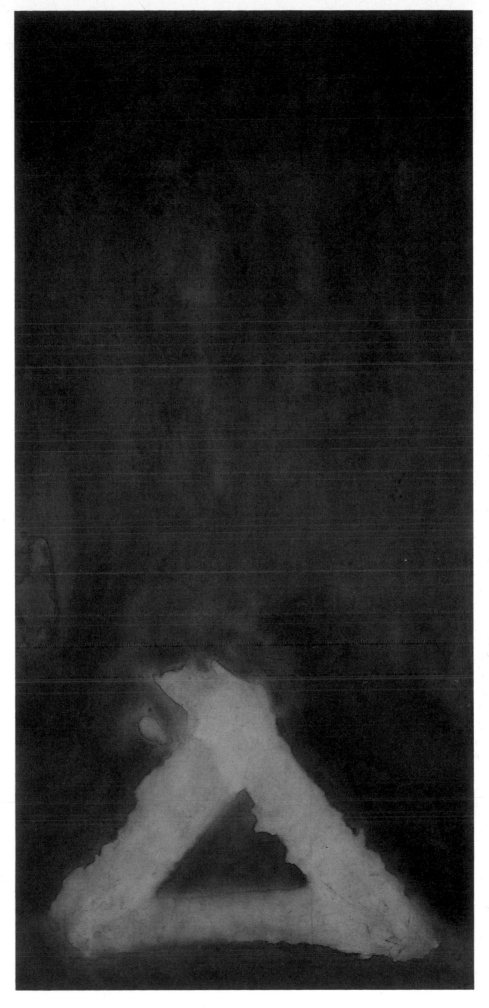

68. TRIANGLE OF VARNISH. 1980.

69. BACK. 1981.

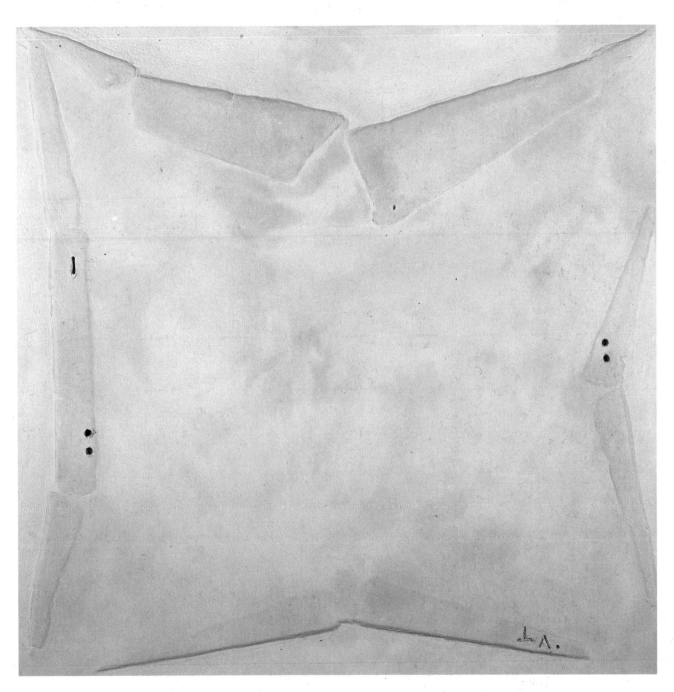

70. FOLDED MATERIAL. 1981.

71.   RED AND BLACK. 1981.

72. TWO WHITE SQUARES. 1981.

73.   BLACK SPIRAL. 1982.

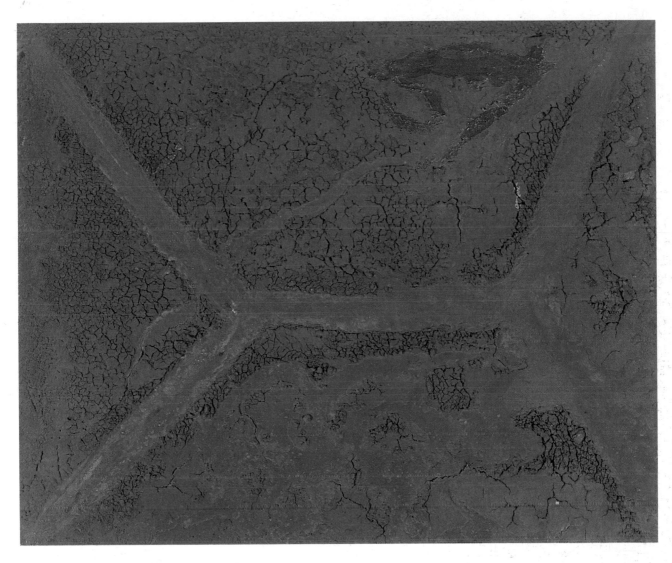

74. BLUE WITH SIGN. 1981.

75. LARGE KNOT. 1982.

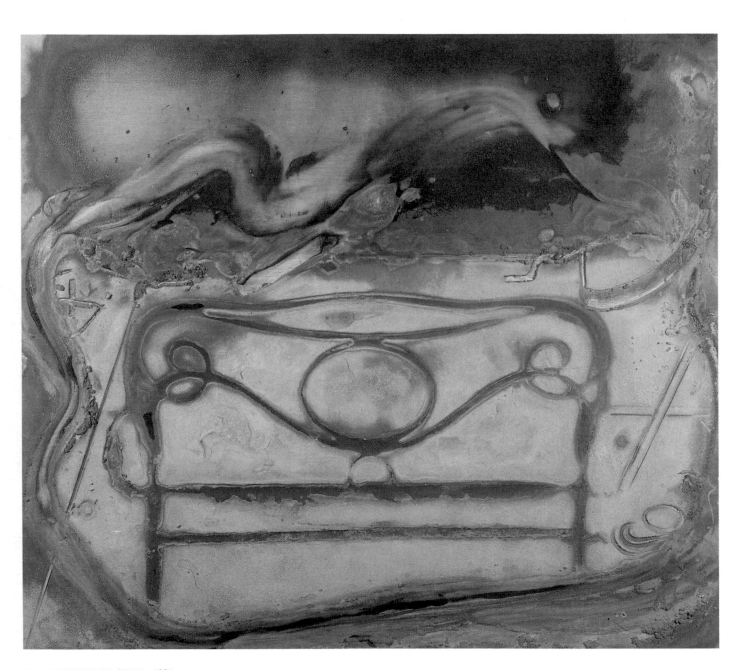

76.   IMPRINT OF SOFA. 1981.

77.   T IN VARNISH. 1981.

78. LEG AND RED CROSS. 1983.

79.   SOLE OF FOOT. 1984.

80.   SILHOUETTE. 1984.

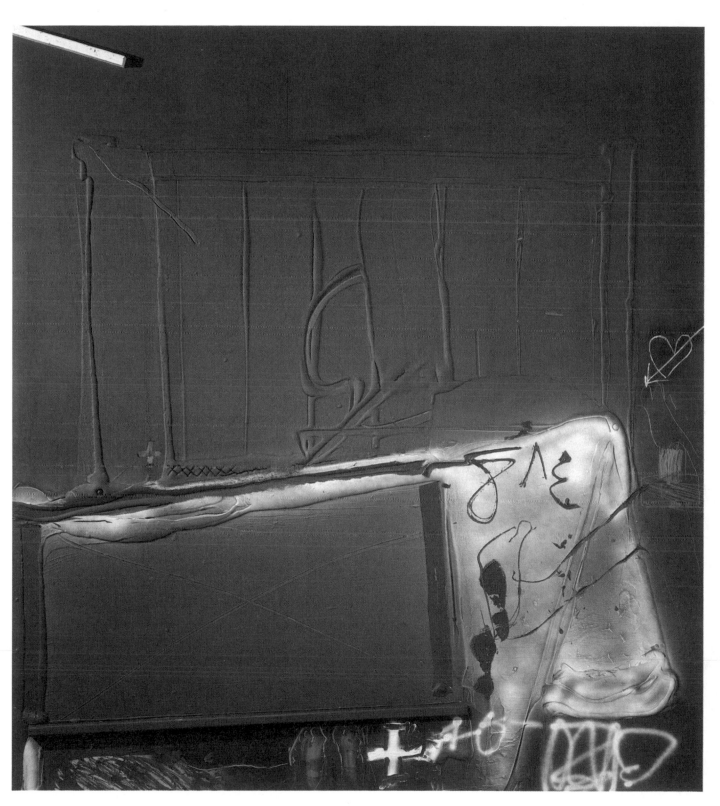

81. BROWN AND WHITE WITH GRAFFITI. 1985.

82. SQUARED. 1986.

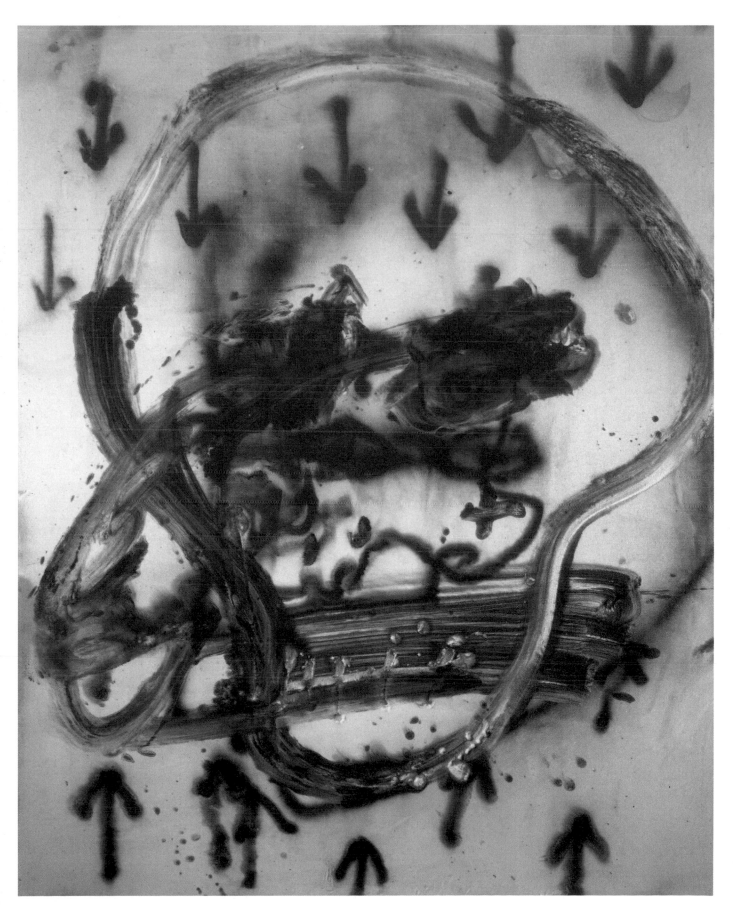

83.   SKULL AND ARROWS. 1986.

84.   WHITE WITH SHUTTER. 1987.

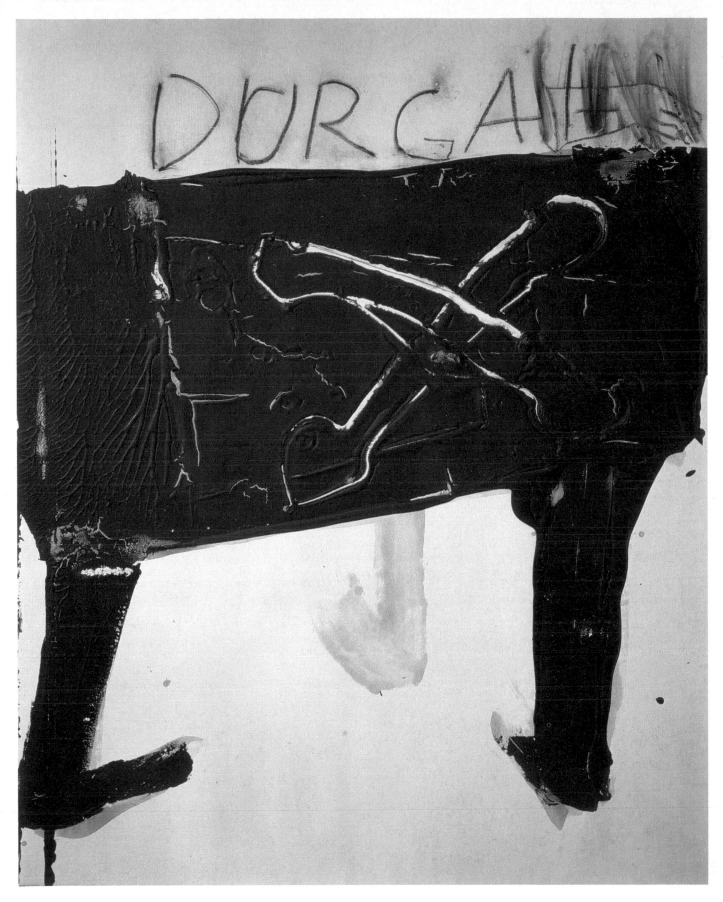

85.   DURGA. 1988.

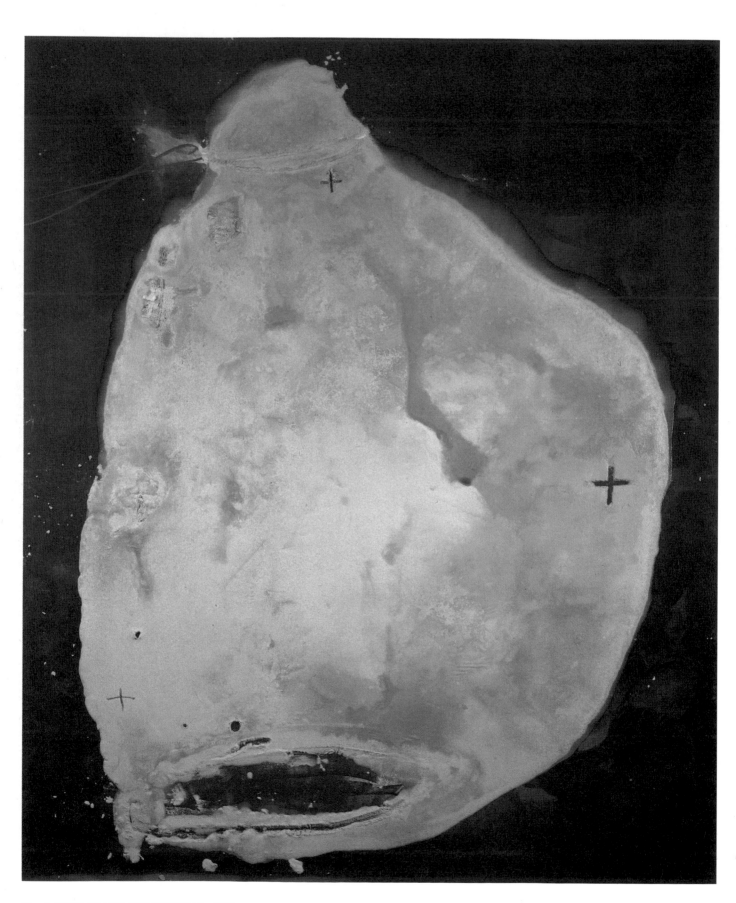

86. LARGE SHAPE OF MATERIAL. 1988.

87. TWO CROSSES. 1989.

INDEX OF ILLUSTRATIONS

33. *Body of Material and Orange-Colored Stains.* 1968.
(Cos de matèria i taques taronges)
Mixed media on canvas, $63^3/_4 \times 51$ in. (162 × 130 cm).
Private collection, Barcelona.

34. *Black and Earth.* 1970.
(Negre i terra)
Mixed media and assemblage on canvas, $51 \times 63^3/_4$ in.
(130 × 162 cm).
Private collection, Valencia.

35. *Emblematic Blue.* 1971.
(Blau emblemàtic)
Mixed media on panel, $63^3/_4 \times 51$ in. (162 × 130 cm).
Private collection, Barcelona.

36. *Blue and Sack.* 1970.
(Blau i sac)
Assemblage on canvas, $42^1/_2 \times 25^3/_4$ in. (108 × 65.5 cm).
Martha Jackson Gallery, New York.

37. *The Catalan Spirit.* 1971.
(L'esperit català)
Mixed media on panel, $78^3/_4 \times 106^1/_4$ in. (200 × 270 cm).
Private collection.

38. *Large Parcel of Straw.* 1969.
(Gran paquet de palla)
Paint and assemblage on canvas, $76^3/_4 \times 106^1/_4 \times 7^3/_4$ in.
(195 × 270 × 20 cm).
IVAM, Valencia.

39. *Mirror and Collage.* 1971.
(Mirall i collage)
Assemblage, $71^1/_4 \times 40^1/_2$ in. (181 × 103 cm).
Private collection.

40. *Two Black Crosses.* 1973.
(Dues creus negres)
Mixed media on canvas, $92^1/_2 \times 59$ in. (235 × 150 cm).
Galerie Maeght, Paris.

41. *Ocher, Brown and White with Fours.* 1972.
(Ocre, marró i blanc amb quatres)
Mixed media on panel, $23^1/_2 \times 28^3/_4$ in. (60 × 73 cm).
Galeria Ravagnon, Venice.

42. *Stage Décor.* 1974.
(Decoració de teatre)
Mixed media on canvas, $76^3/_4 \times 51$ in. (195 × 130 cm).
Private collection.

43. *Sardana-Circle of Feet.* 1972.
(Sardana-Cercle de peus)
Mixed media on panel, $38^1/_2 \times 51$ in. (97.5 × 130 cm).
Private collection, Barcelona.

44. *Earth and Blue.* 1973.
(Terra i blau)
Mixed media on panel, $57^1/_2 \times 44^3/_4$ in. (146 × 114 cm).
Private collection, New York.

45. *Piece of Cloth.* 1973.
(Peça de roba)
Object-assemblage, $39^3/_4 \times 23^1/_4 \times 4^3/_4$ in. (101 × 59 × 12 cm).
Martha Jackson Gallery, New York.

46. *Wardrobe Door.* 1973.
(Porta-armari)
Mixed media on panel, $64^1/_4 \times 40^1/_2$ in. (163 × 103 cm).
Martha Jackson Gallery, New York.

47. *Madman.* 1973.
(Foll)
Acrylic on old Romanesque painting, $23^1/_4 \times 24^1/_2$ in. (59 × 62 cm).
Private collection, Barcelona.

48. *Elbow-Material.* 1973.
(Matèria-Colze)
Mixed media on canvas, $32^1/_4 \times 26$ in. (82 × 66 cm).
Martha Jackson Gallery, New York.

49. *The Ladder.* 1974.
(L'escala)
Mixed media on board, $98^1/_2 \times 118$ in. (250 × 300 cm).
Compañía Telefónica, Spain.

50. *Sí.* 1974.
Mixed media on panel, $76^3/_4 \times 67$ in. (195 × 170 cm).
Martha Jackson Gallery, New York.

51. *Blue Arc.* 1974.
(Arc blau)
Mixed media on canvas, $45^1/_2 \times 35$ in. (116 × 89 cm).
Galerie Beyeler, Basel.

52. *Cork-Oak Grove.* 1975.
(Sureda)
Mixed media on panel, $38^1/_4 \times 51$ in. (97 × 130 cm).
Private collection.

53. *Square on Square.* 1976.
(Quadrat sobre quadrat)
Mixed media on panel, $63^3/_4 \times 63^3/_4$ in. (162 × 162 cm).
Galerie Adrien Maeght, Paris.

54. *Blanket with White Band.* 1976.
(Manta amb banda blanca)
Mixed media on canvas, $76^1/_2 \times 58^1/_4$ in. (194 × 148 cm).
Private collection, Barcelona.

55. *Gray and Orange.* 1977.
(Gris i taronja)
Mixed media on panel, $51 \times 76^3/_4$ in. (130 × 195 cm).
Private collection.

56. *Oval 1-2.* 1978.
Mixed media on panel, $63^3/_4 \times 63^3/_4$ in. (162 × 162 cm).
Private collection, Paris.

57. *"Et amicorum."* 1978.
Mixed media on panel, $108^1/_4 \times 98^1/_2$ in. (275 × 250 cm).
Galerie Pauli, Paris.

58. *Effect of Stick in Relief.* 1979.
(Efecte de bastó en relleu)
Mixed media on cloth and canvas, 55 × 44 in (139.5 × 112 cm).
Private collection.

59. *Composition with India Ink.* 1979.
(Composició amb tinta xinesa)
India ink on cloth, $86^3/_4 \times 82^3/_4$ in. (220 × 210.5 cm).
Private collection, Barcelona.

60. *Effect of Body in Relief.* 1979.
(Efecte de cos en relleu)
Mixed media on cloth and canvas, $77 \times 91^1/_2$ in.
(195.5 × 232.5 cm).
Private collection.

61. *Subject-Object.* 1979.
(Subjecte-Objecte)
Mixed media on blanket and canvas, $78^3/_4 \times 52$ in.
(200 × 132 cm).
Private collection.

62. *Cup.* 1979.
(Tassa)
Mixed media on panel, $25^1/_2 \times 39^1/_4$ in. (65 × 99.5 cm).
Private collection, Barcelona.

63. *Oblique Black Band.* 1979.
(Banda negra en diagonal)
Acrylic on cardboard, $43 \times 62^1/_4$ in. (109 × 158 cm).
Private collection, Barcelona.

64. *Blue and Two Crosses.* 1980.
(Blau i dues creus)
Mixed media on blanket and canvas, $81 \times 57^1/_2$ in.
(206 × 146 cm).
Compañía Telefónica, Spain.

65. *Black on Gray Material.* 1980.
(Negre sobre matèria grisa)
Mixed media on panel, $57^1/_2 \times 44^3/_4$ in. (146 × 114 cm).
Galería Yerba, Murcia.

66. *Curved Forms.* 1980.
(Formes corbes)
Mixed media on panel, $86^3/_4 \times 106^1/_4$ in. (220 × 270 cm).
Private collection, Valencia.

67. *Large Y.* 1980.
(Gran Y)
Mixed media on panel, 76¾×67 in. (195×170 cm).
Private collection, Valencia.

68. *Triangle of Varnish.* 1980.
(Triangle de vernís)
Mixed media on cloth and canvas, 70¾×33¾ in.
(180×85.5 cm).
Private collection, Barcelona.

69. *Back.* 1981.
(Esquena)
Mixed media on panel, 63¾×38¼ in. (162×97 cm).
Private collection, Barcelona.

70. *Folded Material.* 1981.
(Matèria plegada)
Mixed media on panel, 51×51 in. (130×130 cm).
Private collection, Barcelona.

71. *Red and Black.* 1981.
(Roig i negre)
Mixed media on panel, 67×76¾ in. (170×195 cm).
Private collection, Fort Worth, Texas.

72. *Two White Squares.* 1981.
(Dos quadrats blancs)
Mixed media on panel, 76¾×67 in. (195×170 cm).
Private collection, Barcelona.

73. *Black Spiral.* 1982.
(Espiral negra)
India ink and acrylic on cloth and canvas, 130×93¼ in.
(330×237 cm).
Private collection, Barcelona.

74. *Blue with Sign.* 1981.
(Blau amb signe)
Mixed media on panel, 15×18 in. (38×46 cm).
Private collection, Barcelona.

75. *Large Knot.* 1982.
(Gran nus)
Mixed media on panel, 78¾×196¾ in. (200×500 cm).
Private collection, Barcelona.

76. *Imprint of Sofa.* 1981.
(Empremta de sofà)
Mixed media on panel, 67×76¾ in. (170×195 cm).
Private collection, Barcelona.

77. *T in Varnish.* 1981.
(T de vernís)
Mixed media on panel, 78¾×108¼ in. (200×275 cm).
Sally Sirkin Interior Design Collection, Los Angeles,
California.

78. *Leg and Red Cross.* 1983.
(Cama i creu vermella)
Paint and varnish on canvas, 73¾×51 in. (195×130 cm).

79. *Sole of Foot.* 1984.
(Planta de peu)
Paint on canvas, 78¾×67 in. (200×170 cm).
Private collection, Barcelona.

80. *Silhouette.* 1984.
(Silueta)
Varnish and chalk on canvas, 38¼×64 in. (97×162.5 cm).
Private collection, Barcelona.

81. *Brown and White with Graffiti.* 1985.
(Marró i blanc amb grafitti)
Paint on wood, 108¼×98½ in. (275×250 cm).
Private collection, Barcelona.

82. *Squared.* 1986.
(Quadriculat)
Mixed media on canvas, 73¾×67¼ in. (195×170.5 cm).
Private collection, Geneva.

83. *Skull and Arrows.* 1986.
(Crani i fletxes)
Mixed media on panel, 63¾×51¼ in. (162×130.5 cm).
Private collection, Germany.

84. *White with Shutter.* 1987.
(Blanc amb persiana)
Pencil, collage and assemblage on canvas, 98½×67¼ in.
(250×170.5 cm).
Private collection, Barcelona.

85. *Durga.* 1988.
Mixed media on canvas, 63¾×51 in. (162×130 cm).
Galerie Lelong, Paris.

86. *Large Shape of Material.* 1988.
(Gran forma de matèria)
Mixed media on panel, 118×98½ in. (300×250 cm).
Private collection, Paris.

87. *Two Crosses.* 1989.
(Dues creus)
Mixed media on paper, 19¾×26 in. (50×66 cm).
Private collection, New York.